DESERT
HEARTS
AND
HEALING
FOUNTAINS

DESERT
HEARTS
AND
HEALING
FOUNTAINS

Gaining Pastoral
Vocational Clarity

VICTOR L. HUNTER

CHALICE
P R E S S
ST. LOUIS, MISSOURI

Biblical quotations, unless otherwise noted, are from the *New Revised Standard Version Bible*, copyright 1989, Division of Christian Education of the National Council of the Churches of Christ in the United States of America. Used by permission. All rights reserved.

Excerpt on pages 139–40 reprinted with the permission of Scribner, and imprint of Simon & Schuster Adult Publishing Group, from *Letters and Papers from Prison*, revised, enlarged edition by Dietrich Bonhoeffer. Copyright © 1953, 1967, 1971 by SCM Press Ltd.

Excerpts on epigraph page and pages xv and 76 from "In Memory of W. B. Yeats" copyright 1940 & renewed 1968 by W. H. Auden, from *W. H. Auden: The Collected Poems*. Used by permission of Random House, Inc.

Cover art: "Adam and Eve" by Rita Choy Ng, from IMAGE, vol. 72, 1997, published by the Asian Christian Art Association
Cover and interior design: Elizabeth Wright

This book is printed on acid-free, recycled paper.

Visit Chalice Press on the World Wide Web at
www.chalicepress.com

10 9 8 7 6 5 4 3 2 1   03 04 05 06 07 08

Library of Congress Cataloging–in–Publication Data

Hunter, Victor L., 1942-
  Desert hearts and healing fountains : gaining pastoral vocational clarity / Victor L. Hunter.— 1st ed.
    p. cm.
Includes bibliographical references and index.
  ISBN 0-8272-0630-5 (alk. paper)
  1. Clergy—Religious life. 2. Clergy—Office. I. Title.
  BV4011.6.H86 2003
  253'.2—dc21

                                                         2003009626

Printed in the United States of America

For
Phil, Eric, and Jimmy,
conversation partners in ministry
and companions for life

"I am certain of nothing but the holiness of the
Heart's affections and the truth of Imagination."

JOHN KEATS

"In a world without friendship and love,
how could we even begin to understand
the meaning of the sacred?"

STANLEY KUNITZ

Follow, poet, follow right
To the bottom of the night,
With your unconstraining voice
Still persuade us to rejoice;

With the farming of a verse
Make a vineyard of the curse,
Sing of human unsuccess
In a rapture of distress;

In the deserts of the heart
Let the healing fountain start,
In the prison of his days
Teach the free man how to praise.

W. H. AUDEN
"In Memory of W. B. Yeats"

Contents

Acknowledgments

Books have been my conversational partners in ministry. I was always fascinated with the acknowledgments at the beginnings of those books—the people thanked, the influences acknowledged, the support recognized. Not until I published my first book seventeen years ago did I realize how essentially true these acknowledgments are, that they are more than just kind words. Certainly behind this book are many influences, conversations, criticisms, experiences, and insights shared with me by friends and colleagues that have made its writing possible. No person is a theologian, or pastor, alone. You will hear a number of "accents" in my theological diction—and I am grateful to all those who have shaped my speaking.

Among those, I would especially like to thank:

My teacher Rubem Alves, who has made it impossible for me to do theological analysis or reflection without hearing the echoes of a "Brazilian" accent.

My students and faculty colleagues at Phillips Theological Seminary.

The pastors who have participated in continuing education programs through Cotner College and The Disciples Seminary Foundation, where many of the ideas in this book were shared and discussed.

The pastors and church leaders who have shared their stories, lives, and ministries with me over the past twelve years at A Mountain Retreat in Colorado. I especially thank David and Donna Killen, my colleagues at the retreat center, whose hospitality and generosity have contributed enormously to the care, education, and renewal of ministers.

The members of my beloved congregation of the past seventeen years, Evergreen Christian Church (Disciples of Christ), who called me to be their theological pastor and teacher; and Jeannette May, our community's tireless and talented administrative secretary, who helped me keep clarity and focus in my own pastoral vocation.

The Reverend Dr. Kenneth Leech, resident theologian at St. Botolph's in London's East End and gifted spiritual director, whose quiet conversations in the summer and autumn of 2001 helped to nurture me back toward courage and the practice of "subversive orthodoxy" in the chaos, confusion, and contradictions of life's messiness.

My brother Lanny Hunter and my friend Charlie Ottinger, who have sharpened, challenged, and clarified my form of address as both a preacher and a writer.

The Eli Lilly Endowment, which provided me with a National Clergy Renewal Grant that made possible both a period of renewal and time and opportunity for the solitude necessary to complete this book.

Dr. Jon L. Berquist, editor and scholar extraordinaire, whose encouragement and guidance has been invaluable.

My immediate family, without whose love and support I would have no voice or energy to offer the broader church. My wife, Lynette, always "there" and whose faith has not only survived but grown through the ups and downs of thirty-eight years of ministry; my daughter Charisa, pastor and theologian and a challenging conversation partner since her days as an A Level student in London when I was her tutor in the study of religion, and her family; my daughter Heather and her family, whose home in East London has been a place of hospitality for many pilgrims and for me during my extended stay in the summer and autumn of my sabbatical; my son Lance and his wife, Hannah, whose encouragement extended not only to the use of their East London flat as a site for my writing but also to arranging the use of Hannah's parents' home in Ilkley, Yorkshire, for two weeks of uninterrupted writing; and so to the Reverend Roger Fry and his wife, Jean, whose Yorkshire home provided the gift of solitude and silence.

Finally, the dedication of this book acknowledges three friendships without which I do not believe I could have survived in the ministry—or, if I had survived, it would have been as a lesser person and a lesser pastor. They have helped me, from time to time, to "catch a breath," reminding me of Gregory Nazianzen's warning that breathlessness is the principle enemy of the theological/pastoral life. To paraphrase and tinker with some words from Wallace Stegnar's novel, *Crossing to Safety*:

I have been busy, perhaps overbusy, all my life. From the time I first met these friends, our passion had been for ministry, to live up to our vocation, to leave a mark on the world. Our hottest arguments were always about how we could contribute. We did not care about the rewards. We were young and earnest. We never kidded ourselves that we had the political gifts to reorder society or insure social justice. Beyond a basic minimum, money was not a goal we respected...Leave a mark on the world. Instead, the world has left marks on us...I didn't know myself well, and still don't. But I did know, and know now, the few people I loved and trusted. My feeling for them is one part of me I have never quarreled with, even though my relations with them have more than once been abrasive. But we all hoped, in whatever way our capacities permitted, to define and illustrate the worthy life. And the worthy life had something to do with friendship—expanding the circle of friendship in the community of Christ. We have made a stab at it over the past quarter of a century.

Their "fingerprints" are on almost every page of this book; their "touch" is on almost every part of my life.

Victor L. Hunter
Evergreen, Colorado

Preface

This book is a companion and conversation partner for those finding their way—or finding their way back—to parish ministry. It is a book about vocational clarity in the pastorate. It is about the "being and doing" of those committed to answering the call to Christian ministry in the context of the most basic expression of the church—the local congregation. It is about faithfulness to the ordination vows one has either taken in the past or will be taking in the transition from seminary education to the daily and weekly ministry of "word and sacrament."

The pastoral vocation is about speaking the word of God in all life's situations. Pastors must find their voice to be able to speak God's Word among the people of God. Pastors must learn to keep their ordination promises in all of the complexity of following Jesus' injunction to "let our yes be yes and our no be no." The pastoral vocation—listening to the voice that calls and finding our voice to speak to the many and varied circumstances of parish ministry—is to be who you truly are and to live what you truly do with "holy conversation." The conversation takes place between the pastor and God. It takes place between the pastor and the theological and religious tradition. It takes place between the pastor and the laity. It takes place between the church and the culture. This empowering roundtable conversation is a form of table talk in which the pastoral ministry is clarified, the laity are empowered, and the congregation is revitalized in community and mission.

It is important to rethink God-talk and revisit the question of pastoral clarity as the church and its ordained ministers move into the third millennium. It is my conviction that there is a growing forgetfulness of the grammar and syntax of "pastoral speaking." For many pastors, the holy conversation of the pastoral vocation has been abandoned for a foreign language. It has left its native tongue for contemporary, quasi-religious pig Latin. Pastoral speaking is often reduced to pious gossip or, worse yet, polite, politically correct chatter. Pastoral conversation has become little more than clearing our throats.

Because this book is a conversation companion with colleagues who are preparing for the pastoral vocation or are reevaluating their own current practices of pastoral ministry, it must be more "confessional" than "propositional." After all, confession is a primary way in which we "speak Christian," and that is no less true of those of us who are trying to find an authentic pastoral voice. Therefore, this book will be more autobiographical than didactic. It will not be overly concerned with footnotes and references but will draw on my own conversations with the biblical, historical, and theological traditions as well as the "living voices" of fellow sojourners in the pastoral vocation who have blessed, challenged, loved, and fought with me over the past four decades of ministry. It will distill hundreds of hours of conversations, confessions, and prayers with pastors and seminary students who have told me their stories at A Mountain Retreat in Conifer, Colorado. I want to draw you into these conversations to help clarify your own pastoral vocation, because both the church and the world need theological pastors who know that the "head bone is connected to the heart bone." I also hope this book will help congregations understand the relationship between their pastors and their church, including the sometimes messy and ambiguous relationships between elderships, pastor/parish relations committees, pastoral advisory councils, and boards. If successful, pastors and churches will have greater clarity as they live out their respective vocations and can avoid much grief.

* * * * * * *

A funny thing happened to many of us on the way to and from our seminaries.

We came to seminary wanting to love God and serve Jesus in accordance with the "call to ministry" we had received. Necessarily, we entered into the critical study of the faith and its documents. Some came to seminary knowing the basic stories of the faith and traditions of the church. To be sure, this knowledge was often simple and uncomplicated, even naive, perhaps even fundamentalist. It was very important to critically examine the diverse traditions, historical-critical methods, presuppositions, prejudices, and the simplistic answers we had given to difficult, complex, and convoluted human questions and dilemmas. We learned, in Rilke's terms, to "live the questions," and a very important lesson it was. The problem was that we found we could end up with a head full of knowledge, a mind full of questions, and a heart empty of Jesus. And the throat clearing began.

Others arrived at seminary with very little knowledge of the Christian story and its sources, but had a vague interest in the academic study of religion to see where it might lead. Others answered the call to ministry later in life. Since many of our teachers were trained at the great universities in academic theology and its attendant disciplines but had little or no pastoral experience, we benefited from superb biblical, historical, sociological, philosophical, and psychological insights, research, and learning, but this vital intellectual information was gained with limited tutoring into our vocation and pastoral formation. We became refugees from alienated and alienating Christian communities. Too often, seminaries have become minor outposts of major universities rather than communities of intellectual rigor *and* spiritual formation for the pastoral vocation within the church.

This is not to minimize the excellent job seminaries do in theological education, but to acknowledge a failure of cooperation and commitment between churches, judicatories, and seminaries in pastoral formation and vocational clarity. We must find ways of working together that will ensure that formation is occurring as information is accruing, that collegiality is developed as curricula are being studied, and that vocational clarity sharpens along with intellectual acumen. I am interested in encouraging an authentic, open, and continuing discussion between the church and its seminaries. A vital relationship of mutuality will increase the health of the theological academy and its teaching faculty and the church and its pastoral ministers.

A conversation that occurred between D. H. Lawrence and Frieda Weekley, the wife of Lawrence's literature professor, illustrates perfectly various "ways of understanding" that are critical in the study of theology and the formation for ministry. Professor Weekley, a philologist, had invited Lawrence home to dinner. Weekley's German wife, Frieda, did not yet speak English well. After dinner, they asked Lawrence to recite one of his poems. When Lawrence had finished his recitation, he asked Frieda if she understood it. She said, "My husband understood the words but not the poem; I did not understand all the words, but I understood the poem." "Understanding the poem" is part of what I mean when I say the pastoral vocation is a way of speaking. Learning in the pastoral vocation involves:

1. Skills the pastor needs to acquire.
2. Habits the pastor needs to develop.
3. Frameworks within which the pastor works.

Our conversation in this book will focus mostly on the latter two categories.

A word is in order about the book's title. "Desert Hearts" describes the spiritual terrain within which pastors live and work in this new millennium, including the geography of our own souls. The landscapes of our lives and ministries are often parched and arid. The desert—the wilderness—is a lonely, frightening, and trying place. It is fraught with danger and can be a place of death. The wind shifts its sands, covers our tracks, blinds our eyes, and hides the horizon. The stakes are very high for desert pilgrims. But the desert can also be a place of mystery, magic, and beauty. "Healing Fountains" are needed because, given enough water, anything can grow and be a place of transformation. When the fountain wells up from the source of some long-forgotten or hidden spring, even in the harshest of deserts an oasis is created for shelter, sustenance, and beauty.

Pastoral vocational clarity frees the pastor to be and do what the pastor has promised in the ordination vows. It frees and empowers the laity to actually be the church. This book demonstrates the equation:

pastoral vocational clarity + empowered laity = congregational vitality.

Because pastoral vocation is a way of speaking, and because that way of speaking fosters understanding of the poem of Christian faith, W. H. Auden's words come to life in relationship to the pastoral vocation.

Follow, poet, follow right
To the bottom of the night,
With your unconstraining voice,
Still persuade us to rejoice;
With the farming of a verse
Make a vineyard of the curse...
In the deserts of the heart
Let the healing fountain start,
In the prison of his days
Teach the free man how to praise.

The conversations in this book are about deserts of the heart. They are about healing fountains, the courage to follow right to the bottom of the night, and ministry's fundamental purpose: to help us make it through the night. They are about the poetry of the pastoral vocation, that we might again know vineyards, sing praises, and rejoice.

PART ONE

Desert
Reflections
on the
Pastoral
Vocation

CHAPTER 1

Confusions and Current Conditions

Jesus sent the Twelve out two by two on a ministry of preaching, healing, and exorcism with stringent instructions. When they returned, so many people "were coming and going, and they had no leisure even to eat" (i.e., care for themselves). Jesus thus instructed them to "Come away to a deserted place all by yourselves and rest a while."[1]

From the several thousand pastors who have sat with me on the deck of A Mountain Retreat, looking out over the forest toward Riley Peak, it is clear that there is much confusion in the pastoral ministry. Longtime ministers know how many people are "coming and going" in parish life. And not just people as individuals, but groups of people—committees, elders, deacons, boards, judicatory personnel, Sunday school teachers, community organizers, and on the list could go. Each person or group wants or needs something, usually urgently. Spending time with Jesus is a long-forgotten memory. Pace is everything. Rush conquers reflection. Appointments replace prayer. Managing the mess seems mandated over meditating on the mystery. Study is trampled in the stampede of keeping up. Busyness usurps being, or, to transmute the Cartesian principle, "I work, therefore I am." The new arrival from the seminary to the parish comes anticipating the sanctuary and is greeted by a system and set of priorities that threaten to stunt any growth toward vocational clarity and sense of calling that had developed in the academy. "What has Athens to do with Jerusalem?" Indeed. What has the study of academic theology to do with parish ministry? What has running the church to do with preaching, healing, and exorcism? A great deal, to be sure. But finding answers to those questions and implementing them on a day-to-day and week-to-week basis is the domain of pastoral vocational clarity and the task of the truly theological pastor.

The trajectory over the past fifty years of pastoral vocational self-understandings and difficulties can be traced from the findings of Joseph Sittler in the late 1950s through the turmoil of the late 1960s and 1970s to the replacement of modernism by the postmodern thought and methodologies of the late 1980s and 1990s. Sittler argued in his Lyman Beecher Lectures on Preaching at Yale that pastors were suffering from vocational guilt.[2] He spoke of the "maceration of the minister" through too many responsibilities, too various a complex of problems and duties, too unrelenting a drain on emotional and mental resources, and insufficient opportunity to lift the ministerial nose from the parish grindstone. This resulted in the fragmentation of the pastor's vocational identity and purpose, ending in breakdowns and depressions. However, Sittler regarded the real issue at the heart of the matter was a sense of the pastor's vocational guilt. The pastor felt called to an "office" but ended up "running an office." It is hard to maintain a clear vision of vocational identity when the pastor is so seldom doing what he or she considers the call to be.

In the late sixties and early seventies, many pastors began to feel irrelevant and ancillary to the burning issues of the day. The problem was not so much vocational guilt as vocational defeat. Pastors began to search for other ways to express their humanitarian concerns. Many turned to such callings as psychotherapy, social work, and community organizing.

With the coming of postmodernism, the situation today is one of pastoral confusion. Many who have stayed in the parish ministry have sought for all kinds of techniques, even gimmicks, to meet the challenges and confusions of the contemporary scene. "Relevance" continues to be a major issue for many pastors, and the models that continue to be followed for pastoral ministry are those of therapist, community organizer, change agent, religious manager, and CEO of a corporation. It is not guilt or defeat but confusion that marks vocational understandings today.

Jackson Carroll has argued that ministry today calls for reflective practice:

In the exercise of leadership in specific roles of ministry, a fundamental competence needed by clergy professionals is the ability to function as reflective practitioners in a variety of specific roles of ministry. This includes the capacity, in these various roles, to analyze difficult and often novel situations and bring one's beliefs, commitments, knowledge and skills to bear in such a way that one's response is both appropriate to the situation and grounded in a vision of ministry. Such expertise can in part be learned, but only in part. For it must also grow out of a sense of calling from which vision of ministry springs and which also is the ground of the minister's personal authenticity and integrity. It is in the wedding of calling and competence of reflective practice that I believe lies the hope for the vital professional leadership in the shared ministry of the church.[3]

Competent reflective practice is indeed a critical function within the ministerial vocation and needs to be wedded to the "call." But that is just the difficulty for today's pastors in the desert of confusion. What exactly is "the call"? In the short paragraph above, Carroll uses the terms *various roles* or *specific roles of ministry* three times. What *are* the roles, and what *are* the practices that call for reflection? When the calling is confused and the roles of the contemporary pastorate continue to be an unfocused hodgepodge of, no doubt, important and compassionate good works, reflective practice becomes a near impossibility. Gimmicks often replace reflective practice; techniques replace theology; and career replaces vocation. Without vocational clarity, clergy self-understanding gets lost in the immediacy and urgency of demands. In this desert where finding one's way is difficult, confusion can be fatal. The dissolution of vocational clarity is at the heart of the confusion. It poses a dangerous threat to the health and well-being not only of pastors but also of the congregations where they serve. It can result in pastoral ennui and parish enervation. In biblical terms, the wilderness wanderings of Israel come to mind. Forty years of not knowing. Forty years of delayed purpose and fulfillment. Forty years of confusion. The question of the exiles also comes to mind from Psalm 137: "How could we sing the LORD's song in a foreign land?" (v. 4). The failure of the shepherds of Israel in Ezekiel's day, who had neglected the flock of God by forgetting and abandoning the pastoral tasks (Ezekiel 34), is also instructive.

Yet it must be remembered that the desert (or the wilderness, or the exile to a strange land) is spoken of, in biblical terms, in positive as well as negative ways. On the one hand, the desert was a place of trial, testing, deprivation, attack, scarcity of food and water, and death. On the other hand, the wilderness was experienced as a place of closeness and communion with God, where the people could eat at God's table and experience God's care. It was the location of God's revelation on numerous occasions. Finally, it was the site of Jesus' own testing and temptation, and the location in which he formed his identity for his ministry.

There are, therefore, polar images of the desert in biblical narratives. The desert truly is a place of leanness, privation, and danger. But it is also a place for the possibility of revelation, epiphany, preparation, and training for mission and ministry in the broader world.[4] The experience of the desert heart is both challenge and opportunity. Both pastors and congregations must make an honest recognition of the true terrain of ministry to meet the challenge and take advantage of the opportunity.

This is, of course, the challenge to pastoral ministry and the life of the congregation as we move into the third millennium of Christian history. Will this become a time of revelation and renewal for our pastors and their parishes, or a time of faltering into oblivion? One reality is common to the desert experience in the Bible, whether it is spoken of in positive or negative terms: The desert is a place of utter dependence on God.

This is the crux of the matter in terms of pastoral clarity. In 1929 Evelyn Underhill, the great Anglican writer on Christian spirituality, raised a vital issue with Archbishop Lang of Canterbury: "God is the interesting thing about religion, and people are hungry for God. But only a priest whose life is soaked in prayer, sacrifice and love can, by his own spirit of adoring worship, help us to apprehend God." The idea that anyone would be interested in Jesus and the scriptures in the context of the pastoral vocation for any other reason than to serve the people of God and the purposes of God is ludicrous to me. We will return again and again to this issue in the pages that follow.

Desert Markings

I am deeply concerned with the renewal of the church for the sake of its mission to the world. My work in recent years has been devoted to the renewal of the ministry for the sake of the church. My commitment is to the recovery of vocational integrity, identity, and clarity among those of us who are pastors, so that all of us in the *laos* (people) of God can take our part in the mission of God's love for the world. Again, the equation is pastoral vocational clarity + empowered laity = congregational vitality.

Marking 1: Trekking in circles. We are caught in a vicious circle of confusion because the concept of church has become so enculturated. If the church does not know what its identity and mission are, how can the ordained ministry know what it is to be about? And if the ordained ministry of the church does not have vocational clarity, how can the church know what it is and is to be about? This confusion, particularly rampant in American Protestantism, is aptly illustrated by the responses of a Jewish Rabbi, a Roman Catholic priest, and a Protestant minister to a difficult question. The Rabbi responds: "The tradition says!" The priest responds: "The church teaches!" The Protestant minister responds: "Well, it sort of seems to me!" While authoritarianism is inadequate and often despotic, we in the mainline churches are often left with nothing more than random opinions of overworked pastors.

There really is a crisis in pastoral clarity and ecclesial identity, and the crisis in one feeds the crisis in the other. Yet I believe more strongly than ever in the vital importance of Christian community. Perhaps the building of authentic Christian congregations, local churches, genuine communities of faith, is the most important theological, ethical, social, pastoral, and ecumenical work we have before us as we face this new millennium. But what do we mean by church, and what do we mean by pastoral ministry? It simply doesn't do any good to talk about programs, propaganda, agendas, gimmicks, and pep rallies. What is critical is the rediscovery and the renewal of authentic Christian community with faithful pastors who understand the vocation, preachers who know the gospel, teachers who can be interpreters of meaning, and an empowered laity who recognize *they* are the church.

Marking 2: Inadequate camping gear. The Twelve whom Jesus sent into ministry went with not much stuff in their pack but a clear message on their lips—what we have been calling the authentic voice. The faith we confess is an incarnational faith, but our practice of ministry is often decarnational. We speak of gospel realities such as sin and judgment, forgiveness and grace, love and unity, hope and justice, prayer and spirituality. But are these realities incarnate in our clergy and in our communities? "Out of the heart...," Jesus is constantly urging. "The greatest and hardest preparation is within,"[5] said George Herbert. "Only a priest whose life is soaked in prayer…," said Evelyn Underhill. Yet formation is neglected, and we enter the desert overpacked but with inadequate vocational gear. I am reminded of those wartime shops along Oxford Street in London during the hard days of WWII. The display windows were full of beautiful and tasty items. But because of the hard times and rationing, a little sign in the corner of the window said, "These goods not available here." Are the "goods" available in our churches and within our clergy? Do we even know what the "goods" are in this time of vocational confusion?

Marking 3: Faded maps. In a time of confusion and lack of clarity, where do we look for our location, our bearings, and our guidance? When Anglicans run into confusion, they at least have a liturgy in which the gospel is told and retold each Sunday. The Roman Catholics have a long history for some direction. The German Lutherans can point to a deep and vast theological tradition. The members in churches in what were the Iron Curtain countries had a persecution that in its very threat marked out certain boundaries of identity, as do many Chinese Christians. The Latin American churches have a clear mission of liberation and justice in the face of oppressive regimes. But what of North American Protestant churches, which in these desert times have tended toward "shake and bake, make-it-up-as-you-go" church that is often nonliturgical in any historical sense, nontheological, without a clear sense of mission, and, God knows, unpersecuted? Where are the maps?

Marking 4: Shifting sands. Cultural and ecclesial changes are at such a profound depth and breadth at the beginning of this millennium that it is difficult to find a place to stand. The terrain of culture and church keeps shifting beneath our pastoral feet. The mention of just a few of these realities is enough to point to the shifting sands and changing landscapes within which our ministries function and our parishes live:

- The disestablishment of mainline churches
- Declining membership in many congregations
- Concern for the survival of both congregations and denominations
- The disappearance of denominational loyalty
- Clergy shortages
- A growing chasm between ideological camps, including the triumph of "ideology" in all camps as a means of thinking and speaking

- Cultural wars within and without the church
- Biblical and theological ignorance
- The death of Christendom
- The death of modernism
- The radical growth of pluralism, often turned to factionalism
- The reemergence of overt racism and nationalism
- Lack of stable communities
- Detachment from cultural hope
- Lack of consensus on the nature of moral authority, history, and the theory of knowledge
- Personal and social fear

My argument here is not whether these are good or bad developments, and I am sure strong cases can be made for the positive and negative aspects of these various issues. My point is that the desert experience is one of shifting sands.

Failed Desert Strategies

Two ways have emerged in the last part of the twentieth century as responses to desert existence in mainline Protestant churches. Neither of them is viable or faithful.

The first response has been to continue business as usual, fundamentally ignoring the new terrain in which ministry and ecclesial life are now traveling. Often, the "pillars of the church" hold the church up—in both senses of the phrase. The long-term veteran members of the church hold up the church by their giving, their involvement, and their sustaining presence. At other times, however, these same folk can hold up the church by keeping it from advancing into new definitions, new ministries, and new forms of faithfulness in the changing terrain. There can be a retrenchment of the enculturated church, with an effort to keep change at bay by deciding to do the same thing, only "harder and faster." Pastors are often caught in the crossfire of diverse expectations within their own congregational setting. The messages they take on board in their vocational psyche are shaped by these conflicting expectations: We want expert administrators; we want great preaching; we want dynamic youth leaders; we want skilled educators; we want good public relations work in the community; we want social justice campaigners; we want a solid pastoral visitation program; we want a religious "Jack or Jill"-of-all-trades; and on the list goes. This is underscored within congregations by the message: "You know First Church across town is really growing!

Why can't you do that for us!" So pastors continue to attend seminars, get more training, visit the latest church program guru, trying to upgrade their "professional and technological skills" in this direction and that.

I think of this ecclesial retrenchment accompanied by the pastor's frantic search for a new technique for success as "becoming lost in the Protestant ghetto." The Protestant ghetto can manifest itself in a number of ways. From one perspective, it is to continue to be a part of the old-line liberal establishment mentality, usually accompanied by a large dose of nostalgia. This attempt is usually pursued in the name of relevancy by addressing the latest social or global issue without much theological integrity, long-term commitment, or gospel word. Here, the social worker is preferred to the pastor, the change agent to the servant, the therapist to the spiritual friend. From another perspective, the Protestant ghetto is simply a reflection of American cultural values accompanied by a bland and easygoing way of life in which the church doesn't look much different from any other community organization. It simply has pious overtones that challenge nothing, question nothing, proclaim nothing, suffer nothing. Any kind of deep spirituality and life of prayer is virtually nonexistent. The genuine missionary spirit is a matter of embarrassment. Grace is cheap; discipleship is absent; the story is forgotten; there is nothing to teach; and religious timidity or confusion is abundant. Just keep the institution running! What kind of gospel is that?

The other direction many of our churches are opting for is the model of the "contemporary" church espoused by many megachurches. There is a great stampede in this direction because it is seductively attractive, tempting us with the god success— growth in numbers, growth in budgets, growth in services. The real and not-so-hidden agenda and criteria is not the gospel that challenges culture toward repentance and transformation, justice, and holiness, but "meeting the needs of the people." What there is of christology in the megachurches, the church growth churches, the churches that encourage the homogeneous quotient in order to grow and be successful, is not a Jesus who comes as God's silent whisper upon the earth, speaking of and demonstrating the reign of God and finally giving his life on the cross of suffering love, but an individualistic and privatistic Jesus who comes to meet the needs of the people.

Blatantly put, give the people what they want! Give them what they want in worship. Give them what they want in social events.

Give them lots of choices. Cater to their tastes. Such churches are fundamentally nontheological, ahistorical, traditionless, and liturgically shallow. They represent a wholesale sellout of the connection between christology and ecclesiology to pragmatism and the church as consumerism. Ecclesiology is marginalized and demythologized into management and therapeutic models. In this consumerist religion for a consumerist culture, there is a kind of "fast foodism" about the whole enterprise. It might be thought of as McChristianism, or in the terms of Burger King's slogan, "Have it your way." Ignoring the fact that the messianic banquet is not a fast food restaurant, the church becomes understood as simply another place to receive goods and services—the quicker and the easier, the better. The church of the cross, centered in a theology of the cross, is exchanged for the church of the good life of the American dream rooted in a theology of glory. Accommodation to the clanging beat of pop music or the banality of the empty-headed droning of "praise bands," accommodation to the nonexistent attention spans of GenXers, and accommodation to American culture's horror of critical and reflective thought and the place of spiritual wisdom will "only further damage the souls of those the church pursues by such accommodation."[6] Accommodation to an entertainment model of worship makes one wonder if there will be anything left from the rich historical worship traditions to sustain people through sickness, sorrow, suffering, and death. I believe the day is not far off when "accommodation" foisted off as evangelism, and "meeting the needs of the people" foisted off as gospel, will be seen for what they are: fishing with broken nets.

In one direction there is pure ghetto. In the other direction there is pure boulevard. If the Protestant ghetto offers cheap grace, the contemporary "give them what they want" consumerist church offers an imitation of cheap grace. It is like the $4.00 Rolex watches—a cheap imitation of the real thing, but it looks good on the outside. Is there another option, which, once upon a time, was called "The Way?"

Desert Paths

In this time of disestablishment for North American churches; in this time of post-Constantinian, postdenominational, postliberal, postmodern, postauthoritarian confusion; in this time of cosmic ecclesial paradigm shifts and rejections; in this time of nonreflective, "give them what they want," shake-and-bake church experience; in this time of pluralism-gone-to-seed factionalism; in this time of vocational and ecclesial lack of clarity; in this time of desert wandering and wondering, I would argue for a way ahead for the community *en Christo* that was once called "The Way," to a new sojourning vision of a church at once *catholic* and *confessing*. We have the opportunity in the desert experience of moving from a Christianity of place to a Christianity of way, and from a Christianity of possession to a Christianity of relinquishment. Leaving behind the place of power, privilege, hierarchy, imperialism, patriarchy, racism, and wealthy comfort, we can actually begin to pay attention to the geography of the terrain of the Way's journey. In this Way, our theological explorations that accompany our faith sojourn will have to become radically contextual, paying careful attention to the local. But the local will not be parochial because there will be a genuine and authentic dialogue across all boundaries, including the boundaries of faith and unbelief, as has always been when the church is truly catholic and confessing.

The Way Catholic

What do I mean by a church catholic as we move into the third millennium? At its heart, I mean, of course, the true universality of the church, not a universality that is defined by those in power and with wealth. I mean the ecumenical church and the unity of the church. I mean the church with a history and histories, with a tradition and traditions. In Hans Kung's thought, I mean a church that can both remain what it is and become what it ought to become. The gospel did not begin with us and will not end with us. The catholicity of the church refers to the whole church, the church universal, and includes all the years of its history and its developments, including both its bright side and its shadowy side. Our faith is catholic. Our name is catholic. Our creeds are catholic. Our gospel is catholic. Our sacraments are catholic. Unless, that is, we are governed by narrow and sectarian ideology (from the left or the right) rather than by generous and universal gospel. The catholic vision or path can free us from a parochial narrowness, blindness, and exclusivity. It will free us from the factionalism of special interest groups, one-issue–oriented theologies, cultural war ideologies used as litmus tests for conversation, and socioeconomic and cultural domestication of the faith. The church catholic should broaden our horizons and deepen our sensitivities and expand our suffering involvement in mission. A church that is catholic recognizes that the community *en Christo* transcends all natural and historical boundaries and will live to manifest that. A church that is catholic recognizes that the whole world—the *cosmos*, indeed the universe of all creation—is the object of God's suffering love. A church catholic hears its confession of faith as one voice in many languages, forms, and cultural expressions—one body in *diaspora*. Catholicity is connected to the call of Jesus Christ to the whole world and the sending of the called into the whole world.

You, of course, hear in this affirmation the third article of the Nicene Creed: "We believe in the one, holy, catholic and apostolic church." In these "marks" of the church, catholicity is joined by the marks of oneness, holiness, and apostolicity. The oneness of the church is in Jesus Christ and reflects our Lord's prayer that "they all may be one." Unity is not to be understood sociologically, organically, or parochially, but theologically. It is not an ideology or a principle to be achieved, but a gift that is given. According to Ignatius of Antioch, martyred around 110 C.E. : "Where Jesus Christ is, there is the catholic church." The unity of the church is found in the One who *calls* the church...the "one Lord Jesus Christ," according to the Chalcedonian formulation. If we as Christians take our "ministry of reconciliation" as a way of being in the world, and take it seriously, then we cannot be blasé in the face of factionalism, sectarianism, and a plethora of institutionalisms that are distrustful, hateful, and arrogant. We live in very practical ways the expression of hope that is the *telos* (end and fulfillment) of God's reunification of all that is divided, separated, marginalized, and alienated.

How can we speak of the holiness of the church when it is made up of sinners like you and me—sinners morally, ethically, religiously, intellectually, and doctrinally? When I speak of the holiness of the church, I am not referring to the politics of purity or the fantasy of "separatist purity." Do we not confess that we are Christians because we are sinners who need forgiveness? Just as unity must be understood theologically rather than organizationally, holiness must be understood theologically rather than perfectionisticly. The term itself means to be set apart for a special purpose and service to God. The setting apart is not an end in itself. The *ecclesia*, the "called out," is not an end in itself. The calling and the setting apart are for the purpose of being sent back into the world of God's primary love. Holiness, therefore, has to do with the mess, the mystery, and the mass. We see the mess we are in and that God was not aloof from the mess but entered the mess. This is the mystery of the incarnation. When we recognize this mystery and are held by it, we celebrate the mass. And the mass means to be sent back into the world. The holiness of the church is in the One who entered the mess and calls the church. And his holiness was lived in the midst of the unholy for the sake of God's suffering love—among tax collectors and sinners. This brings us back to the church as the Way that is *en Christo* for the sake of the world of God's love. Holiness is not to escape the world, but to be in the world while not being of the world. We are reminded here that we are *simul justus et peccator*—at one and the same time justified and sinful. The holiness of the church is impossible without the humility of the church. The choice here is between the politics of purity and the community of compassion. Jesus practiced indiscriminate (promiscuous) eating, healing, and socializing. His holiness often violated the purity codes with inclusive compassion.

The apostolicity of the church is clearly envisioned in Paul's affirmation: "You are citizens with the saints and also members of the household of God, built upon the foundation of the apostles and prophets, with Christ Jesus himself as the cornerstone."[7] This means that Christian origins and the apostolic witness will always be of vital importance to the Christian way. The church catholic is the church apostolic—the church and the faith are historical realities, not disembodied ideas. Rather than apostolic witness, the church today too often engages in pious small talk. To be apostolic is to be historically connected through collective memory to the origins of the church. This means being a hearing and responding fellowship to Holy Scripture. It means being informed by the historic creeds, which are

> nothing more or less than an ordered summary of what their formulators understood to be "the basics"; they are rudimentary systems of theology signifying what is believed to be the essence of the apostolic tradition…A faith whose foundations lie in historical event does not despise some organizational ordering of the community that attempts, through the passing on of the credentials of authority from one generation to the next, to safeguard the continuity of the present and future with the normative past.[8]

The creeds, of course, both define and distort and are products of their own historical circumstances. But the scriptures and the creeds are part and parcel of the historical quest for a continued connectedness between a living church and a normative original. Ultimately, the apostolicity of the church is connected to the search for the voice of the One who calls the church into being, and, therefore, to a careful listening to the first witnesses. In Jerome's words, "Not to know the scriptures is not to know Christ."[9]

I must offer here one caveat, the content of which will have to be explored by the multitudinous communities that make up the catholic way in all their varied contexts. All of these "marks of the church" have a shadow side, not the least of which is the shadow of Roman imperial rule that fell over some of the early councils. But to be a church catholic is to be able to live with the ambiguities of light and shadow that make up the history of a living community. The crisis that is the judgment *(krisis)* of God always begins with the household of faith and its misuses and abuses of power in the critical analysis of the received tradition. At the same time, these "marks" have been provided to help Christians in each succeeding generation to distinguish the essence from the accidents of the Christian way in the world. As Douglas John Hall argues, "At a time when there is once again a strong danger that Christianity will disappear into a thousand factions with colliding emphases and ideologies, such traditions ought to be considered providential in a quite literal sense."[10]

For example, compare these historic marks with much of today's experience.

Rather than the one historic church, we have what I have called "shake-and-bake" churches in which there is no acknowledged history, no sense of tradition, and an intolerable thinness of theological and spiritual wisdom. There is the attempt, even within single congregations, to have a church catering to every sociological group and every special interest lobby. Did we not learn at Antioch that when we form separate tables it just isn't church anymore? Apparently not. For we have had some of all of it: black church/ white church, straight/gay, traditional/contemporary, man/ woman, iconoclast/icon, social issue/religious issue, youth/ elderly, Xer/Boomer, conservative/progressive, ad infinitum, ad nauseam. We must learn to talk across boundaries, believe across generations, share wisdom across cultures.

Rather than the holiness of the church, defined by the community of compassion, we have the relevant church, defined by the "with it" experience.

Rather than the catholic, ecumenical, and universal church, we have the local church gone to seed, the parochial church doing its own thing, forgetful of the prayer of Jesus.

Rather than the apostolic church, we have the contemporary church built around the personality cults of its pastors, the hype of it superstars, and the "friendliness" of its congregations, not to mention one-issue theology and litmus-test political correctness.

In this time of the disestablishment of the churches, the goal of the church catholic would not be to move toward the reestablishment of ecclesial power, but the renewal of the catholic vision. This vision will renew our understanding of what it means to "be church"—not just a voluntary organization for doing good things and meeting the needs of the people. Renewing our understanding of the body of Christ will refocus the church's life together in its constituting act—the holy eucharist, the table of the Lord. Here we come to the deepest mystery and the greatest meaning of the Christian faith. The eucharistic bread is the body of Christ. We are in a realm in which bread is body and body is church. Incarnation and ecclesiology are reunited. The catholic vision reminds us we are not Manichean or Platonist, pitting the spiritual against the physical, but Christian. The catholic vision calls us to be more Augustinian than Pelagian. The catholic vision reminds us that we are more Jewish than Western. It calls us to more of an Elizabethan spirit than a Victorian spirit—we, as human beings, really are *humus*, of the earth. The catholic vision moves us away from the ideational and ideological toward the mystical and sacramental.

And what is the point of this catholic, sacramental vision? To bring together again the body of Jesus of Nazareth broken and offered in history, with the body of Christ in the eucharistic bread broken and offered in presence, with the body of Christ the church broken and offered in service. In this realm of mystery in which bread is body and body is church, and both are sacramental and based on the word of the Word incarnate, we learn that all is offering, all is participation in the body and blood of Christ, all is connected to the suffering love of God and the sufferings that are present in the world, and all of life is worship.

And this unites the church catholic with the church confessing.

The Way Confessing

The word *confession* means fundamentally "to acknowledge together." To be a people of Christian faith in a disciple community is "to confess"—to acknowledge together through the ways we live, speak, suffer, celebrate, serve. Confession is not simply religious self-expression or enthusiastic and joyful affirmation in words. It is both word and deed, both personal and communal. It is the church's vocation, and it is not an option. While the word *confession* is used in two ways in the Christian tradition—confessing sin and confessing the faith—my focus here is on the desert path of confessing the faith as a confessing church. I use it in the sense of the received tradition from the confessing church in Germany as distinct from the German Christians of that era.[11]

Douglas John Hall has effectively called our attention to five things that are required to be a confessing church.[12]

1. The confessing church must be a true community of Christian disciples—not pseudo-community, voluntaristic association, social club of like-minded people, establishment institution, tax-exempt organization. Rather, the confessing church is a hearing and responding *koinonia* of intentional commitment to the way and word lived and spoken by Jesus of Nazareth.

2. The confessing church always makes its confession of faith in a specific context. It does not just "broadcast" its faith in general. It sees and understands propaganda and its methods to be antithetical to "speaking Christian." The confessing church understands there is no such thing as "generic spirituality" or "generic confession." It involves specific, worldly engagement with the sufferings of its current time and place in history.

3. There is always a content to Christian confession in a confessing church. Confession is not abstractions about general good, truth, and beauty. "For we do not proclaim ourselves; we proclaim Jesus Christ as Lord and ourselves as your slaves."[13] The church's confession is rooted in the core narrative of the gospel—the *evangel*. Without identity, a person is "nobody's nothing,"[14] according to Anna Freud. Without identity in Jesus of Nazareth, the church is "nobody's nothing," which, ironically, leads it to try to be "everybody's everything." Only from the depth of the content that the church confesses can the church engage in mission and dialogue in a pluralistic world. The content of the confession is not a matter of dogmatic pride, but of clarity of identity. The core narrative of the gospel is the lens through which the confessing church looks at and interacts with the world and interprets existence toward meaning.

4. The confessing church offers correction for what is wrong with both the church and the world. Judgment always begins with the household of God. The confessing church knows the church is always in need of correction, reformation, and renewal. If the church's "way" of being in the world is confession, it implies that the church is always on a journey, always a work in progress, having never arrived. But not only does the church

need correction, so does the world in specific contexts in which it is encountered. As the formulators of the Barmen Declaration[15] knew, true confession involves not only affirmations but corrections, not only beliefs but damnations, not only the "we believe" but the "we reject." And this is extremely difficult for a church whose pastors, as Carlyle Marney observed, "are unable to say 'boo' to a church mouse, let alone damn to a culture that is antichrist."[16] In order to contextually shape the good news for the culture in which the church confesses, it must name what the bad news is.

5. A cross will always be at the center of the confessing church. This is the starting point of the Christian faith, and Jesus on the cross is the revelation of God's identification with all people who suffer. We have been baptized into "Jesus' death." To be a suffering church, something almost anathema to North American visions of a "successful church" or a "surviving church," is to be a confessing church.

Community, context, content, correction, and cross. A church catholic and confessing bears these marks and is rooted in the voice of the One who calls it and whom it confesses. But how is that call and confession to be heard and made? It will take pastors and people who can move beyond the confusion to some sense of clarity of the pastoral vocation and the church's vocation. It will certainly take pastors who can read both words and worlds. The way ahead to such clarity will be the focus of the remainder of this book. But first we must consider some of the desert dilemmas in which pastors are actually working in today's general context.

Desert Dilemmas

A dilemma is a predicament that defies a satisfactory solution. It certainly defies an easy solution. Yet in a technological culture undergirded by the American propensity for both problem solving and instant gratification, the temptation to find solutions, or "things that will work," is great. The piles of (junk) mail that come across my desk daily are filled with offers of readily available solutions to almost all pastoral problems. There is a seminar for everything, offering "the latest how-to" answer for almost all parish issues. Most of the issues addressed are in those areas of ministry that can be measured, places we can get "counted": budgets, building programs, attendance, church growth, jazzing up the worship, and so forth. I am sure there are some good ideas being presented. My concern is with the tendency to approach ministry as "technique," or ministry as "problem solving." This approach continues to lead us away from the more difficult and murky vocational task of meanings, interpreting our way through the desert, making sense of our lives before God, confronting "the world, the flesh, and the devil" (in the words of "The Great Litany," *The Book of Common Prayer*[17]), and pointing to sightings of Jesus among us.

John Snow has called our attention to the fact that "Christianity is a terrible problem solver. It is not a spiritual technology nor a social or psychological technique; it runs into little but frustration and despair whenever it sees itself in this light."[18] If we can accept the idea that there really are no quick solutions, clever gimmicks, or ministerial techniques that can move us through the desert journey or touch our desert hearts, we are free to settle into a reflective and meaning-making mode in face of the dilemmas we confront regarding pastoral confusion.

While the list could be extended, I would like to suggest five dilemmas that are examples of the kind of general context we find ourselves in today.[19]

Dilemma One

Pastors are being called to lead a new church in a new day for all the reasons mentioned earlier in this chapter. Most of the "props" are gone. Many believe the cultural and religious situations in terms of paradigm shifts are as profound at the beginning of the twenty-first century as they were at the beginning of the sixteenth century.[20] Perhaps they are even more complex. In the church there is a call for new styles of leadership, new models of church, new understandings of mission, new methods of worship and liturgy.

On the one hand, pastors have been accused, and often rightly so, of creating lay dependents. We have sometimes modeled controlling power rather than serving power. Any approach to leadership that smacks of authoritarianism is broadly rejected. There is a form of egalitarianism in American churches that suggests that any idea from anyone on any subject is as good and true and valuable as anyone else's, regardless of experience, training, preparation, and reflective abilities. Whatever anyone offers has as much merit as whatever anyone else offers; therefore, there is no real need for interpreters or intermediaries to guide thinking, evaluate ideas, or develop action. This has resulted not only in a suspicion of leadership but in a fear of leading. To be sure, every person is valuable and should be heard, but some ideas are better than others, some interpretations more accurate, some values more enduring, some actions more appropriate.

On the other hand, trained pastors react to a consumer society that wants to dictate the nature and delivery of "religious services." While some clergy seem to welcome the consumerist concept (I remember a pastor delighting over his GenX–oriented service, saying, "It doesn't even look anything like a church," apparently with no sense of irony), other clergy see the consumer trend as self-destructive. The gospel simply cannot be rendered by quick fixes, instant satisfaction, give-them-what-they-want approaches, and sound bite platitudes.

Dilemma Two

The second dilemma is something of the other side of the coin of the first dilemma. Congregations have become more educated, sophisticated, complex, and pluralistic. Many do want professionals with competence.

On the one hand, many pastors have gone after these skills, trying to develop competence in numerous areas. They search for listening skills, therapeutic skills, management skills, personnel skills, sociological/social science skills, business skills, fundraising skills, technological skills, and so forth. In fact, it could easily be argued that a good number of clergy know more about these skills than developments in biblical studies, the traditions of the church, or doing theology.

On the other hand, the church needs interpreters of meaning, preachers of the gospel, liturgists, scholars, teachers of the faith, and theologians whose lives are committed to the parish ministry. It needs women and men who can, as I have said, read both written texts and human textures, words and worlds. In short, it needs pastors with a clear understanding of the pastoral vocation. It needs the recovery of the wisdom tradition and a rediscovery of the meaning and the practice of the prophetic tradition. The church catholic and confessing in today's world, if it is to reflect Christ's ministry and not just bourgeois religion in its lowest common denominator expression, needs, in Hall's words,

> a learned laity and learned pastors. Not, it is hoped, men and women who are made pompous by their learning, but persons in whom those who hunger and thirst for truth will be able to recognize something approaching depth of understanding and curiosity. There is already such a slide

toward anti-intellectualism and religious *kitsch* that the trend can be altered only with the greatest of effort. Perhaps for the majority it cannot be altered. Nevertheless, the effort must be made, because the alternative is the further trivialization of the faith, and, finally, its relegation to sheer religious froth. And that is a fate too melancholy to contemplate for a faith that could move the intellects and hearts of an Augustine, an Aquinas, a Luther, a Simone Weil, a Dietrich Bonhoeffer, and countless others.[21]

It is ironic that many pastors:

- know and can talk through all the stages of death and dying, but do not know how to be and pray with someone who is dying.
- can discuss the theories of depth psychology and transference, but haven't the faintest idea of the practice of being a spiritual friend or a spiritual director.
- are skilled at doing a sociological analysis of the urban crisis, but are ignorant of the nature of Christian community in the tenement churches in early Rome.
- speak eloquently in economic terms of the death of the family farm and the struggle of rural churches to survive, but have no concept of whether Jesus' death and resurrection makes any difference to that situation.

Dilemma Three

Over the past few years a powerful new interest has developed among a fairly broad spectrum of the population in "spirituality"—often what might be called "individual spiritualities." There are times when the pastor's competence is being questioned not only with regard to his or her role as clergy, but in terms of his or her very competence before God. It can be felt in the number of people turning to individual gurus, arcane or exotic spiritualities, Eastern religions, personal growth groups, angelology, and the myriad numbers and kinds of self-help and self-actualization books.

On the one hand, the pastor has spent many years in education. We have studied, read, and taken courses in the Bible, philosophy, history, theology, ethics, pastoral care and counseling, and various traditions of spirituality.

On the other hand, being experienced or "soaked" in the practice of contemplative prayer, meditation, and the spiritual disciplines is another matter. After all, we are too busy for the time serious spiritual practices take! Equally as difficult is being able to have conversation in a helpfully articulate manner about faith and its practices and the numinous and its mystery.

Professor Diogenes Allen speaks of his own struggle in this area in a particularly helpful and radically honest manner:

> What troubled me at that time is not easy to put into words even now. I found myself wondering again and again what it would be like actually to live every moment of one's life with an awareness of God. I do not mean that I actually wanted to live that way, because it would be quite daunting—this constant awareness of being in God's presence. Still, I was troubled by my ignorance. In spite of my religious faith, the ability to preach sermons and to give lectures that were as good (or bad) as the next person, most of the time God seemed remote. Although I had a doctorate in philosophy and theology, and had read a lot of books, I did not really know what it meant to have an awareness of God in daily life, or how one went about achieving it. How is it that in all my church attendance and advanced education I had not learned such an elementary matter?[22]

How hauntingly familiar his reflection is to me, perhaps to you as well.

Another angle on this dilemma is the current emphasis on the individualistic aspect of the new quest coupled with a seeming disinterest in justice issues. A Confessing Church pastor of long ago, Dietrich Bonhoeffer knew and said that the rhythm of transformation is prayer *and* the doing of justice. On the one hand, as a pastor I know personally the gap between the vision and the reality of cultivating the spiritual life within myself and my parish, and I know the current interest tends toward privatism. On the other hand, I know a Jesus of the gospels concerned with such social realities as kingdom, community, marginalized people, wealth, and the poor.

Dilemma Four

The church is the body of Christ broken in the world for six days in service. It is raised again in unity on the first day in sacramental worship. What has been scattered is gathered together. What has been in *diaspora* has come home. The dilemma for pastors is that the very ground of the constituting act of the Christian congregation, holy worship, has itself become fractured through what one might call "the worship wars." What once brought the people of God together in solidarity now drives them into separate camps. This is not, of course, a new problem. Cultural containers for carrying the gospel have been an issue in the Christian community from the beginning.

Some have called any form of "traditional" worship "unintelligible gobbledygook" to the "unchurched." Others have said, "You will change the worship service over my dead body!" Worship "styles" (an interesting contemporary concept in itself if there ever was one!) have become a matter of hot debate and incredible tension. One solution has been to try to provide a style for every occasion, a service for every taste, a gathering for every sociological and age subgroup. "There is neither Jew nor Greek, slave nor free, male nor female, for you are all one in Christ Jesus" has been exchanged for "you are a seeker or a belonger (presumably those who consider themselves Christians or church members are no longer seekers!), a traditionalist or a contemporary, an X-er or a Y-er, a D-er or a boomer, for you are all multifarious and entitled to your own tastes or lack thereof in Christ Jesus Polymorphous."

On the one hand, liturgical renewal is important. On the other hand, much of what passes as contemporary worship is not liturgical renewal.

On the one hand, "contemporary worship" may express the best missionary impulse in terms of cultural containers for the gospel. On the other hand, "contemporary worship" in many cases may have emptied the container of gospel altogether through liturgical bankruptcy.

On the one hand, Christian worship should be able to speak and sing the gospel in a multilingual, multicultural world, moving us beyond the parochialism of our own limited experience. On the other hand, a moronic hodgepodge of bad-taste drivel using the sweet name of Jesus should not be passed off under the guise of worship as gospel.

There is simply no place for the pastor to hide from these tensions because they revolve around the central act of the whole community's gathering. The pastor is sure to offend in this area. New ways ahead are being sought, explored, and thought about. In the meantime, pastors should be neither gullible nor rigid. I find it helpful to speak to the congregation concerning its public worship in terms of content on the one hand and aesthetics on the other. I try to accompany this with a revisitation to the spot where the debate begins: What is worship?

Another thing to keep in mind is that form allows for flexibility, structure for creativity, continuity for change. Ask any poet or musician. In other words, I believe the historic liturgical consensus provides the best narrative structure for flexibility in the language and expression of worship. I love the scene in the musical *Fiddler on the Roof* when the question is asked as the fiddler skips across the steep, sloping, dangerous roof: "What holds him up?" The resounding answer is "Tradition!" We do need the creativity of fiddling around, but it is only possible because we are held up by tradition. Recently I was with a group of pilgrims in Western Asia Minor. We visited the ruins of an old synagogue and thought of our common heritage with Judaism, the sufferings and the pogroms, and the pain inflicted by anti-Semitism, some of it inflicted by Christians. We shielded ourselves from the late afternoon sun in the shade of the preserved synagogue wall and listened as one of our group, a classical violinist, played the Kaddish (the Jewish prayer sung or said in mourning after death). We sat in silence as the last strains of the music faded into the heavy air. We worshiped. It was not traditional. It was traditional. It was not contemporary. It was contemporary. Should we not weep for the wars over worship?

Dilemma Five

To put the final dilemma bluntly: money and ministry, career and vocation, employment and faithfulness.

On the one hand, we need to stay employed, make enough money to attend to our families, develop professionally, and take care of ourselves. This is not selfish in any way. It is part of self-care and being responsible. Downcast leaders and irresponsible citizens do not make very credible witnesses to an enlivening presence and the teacher of the Sermon on the Mount.

On the other hand, we have responded to a call and are living out a vocation, not a professional career. Pastors are the servants of Christ. Current cultural values do not determine success and failure in this vocation, although we often act as if they do. On the one hand, the pastoral vocation is more than a living. On the other hand, it is less than a life. Nonetheless, keeping focus on who we are before God and what we were called to be and do must not blur in the shortsightedness of career interests.

CHAPTER 2

Compasses and the Journey

An essential tool for desert travel, with its lack of roads, lack of familiar landmarks, and ever-shifting sands, is a compass. What are the compasses for pastors whose terrain is desert, whose travels are through the wilderness, and whose address is permanent exile? I wish to use the term metaphorically in four of its meanings.

The Meanings and Functions of Compasses

When we speak of a compass, we usually think of the instrument that is used for finding our direction, for locating true north, in order to get our bearings and decide which way we need to go. The journey is not, of course, in the compass, but the traveling of the one who uses the compass. Simply reading the compass will get you nowhere. Nonetheless, this direction-finding, needle-pointing, bearing-orienting instrument is essential to desert travel, including pastoral travel in desert terrain.

A compass is also an instrument that is used for measuring distances and drawing circles. It has two arms joined at one end, one arm of which serves as a pivot or stationary reference point. Used properly, it allows one to mark off accurate locations and well-measured boundaries. Again, the locations and the boundaries are not in the compass, but in the medium that is being marked off and calculated. A stationary point is a valuable tool in pastoral work when many people are pointing to a plethora of central points. Marking off boundaries is also critical.

Compass is also a term that means the limits or the range of something, as in "the compass of education." What is the compass of the pastoral vocation? What is the range, and what are the limits? What is within the purview of pastoral ministry? An understanding of personal, professional, and vocational limits is critical to pastoral vocational clarity. When one does not know one's personal limitations or professional training limitations in desert travel, it can be fatal. If one is leading a group through the desert, it can be fatal to the group.

In music, the term compass means the lowest and highest note attainable by a voice. We also use the term *range* in this way. I choose to include it here for a slightly different reason. Compass, in this sense, has to do with self-knowledge. The musician must know his or her own voice, including its range or compass. The pastoral vocation also involves this kind of self-knowledge. The pastor needs to know the range and compass of the vocation itself. Then the pastor needs to know his or her own voice and its compass within the vocation. Knowing the compass of the voice is the very basis of the concept of vocation.

The use of these various images and functions of the compass is very important to gaining clarity in the pastoral vocation.

- A pastor needs to find his or her bearings within ministry in order to gain perspective and mark out directions into the future. Without this kind of compass, "traveling in circles" or "riding off in all directions" are true dangers, resulting in and producing confusion.
- A pastor needs a stationary reference point in order to mark off boundaries and set limits to pastoral movement. A lack of boundaries and limits results in and produces confusion.
- A pastor needs to know the purview of the pastoral vocation, what it includes and doesn't include. Failure to recognize the range of the vocation results in and produces confusion.
- Inability to know and claim one's own voice within the pastoral vocation results in and produces confusion.

Historic Markers as Helpful Compasses

Two historical markers provide such compasses for pastoral clarity in desert travel. The first historical marker is composed of the four elements involved in a "call to ministry": (1) the personal element, (2) the charismatic element, (3) the institutional element, and (4) the democratic element. The call to pastoral ministry is personal, but it is not private. Individuals respond, but it is not individualistic. It involves far more than a vague desire to do good and serve God. It consists of more than good intentions. It goes beyond the desire to "save one's own soul" and "solve one's own problems." The call to ministry involves the personal, the historic, and the institutional. Herein we make use of the compass imagery in its various aspects.

The personal element involves all that we are and all that we are becoming. It involves our own narrative history, our conversion and our commitments, and that intensely personal experience of "hearing" the call in whatever form or manner the call expresses itself. It need not be either dramatic or mundane. It also involves the nature of our faith and our experience of the faith community.

The charismatic element of the call to ministry involves the "gifts" we have been given. To some extent, our gifts (and the self-knowledge of them, the compass of them) will influence the kind and nature of our ministry. Not all "called to ministry" are called to the ordained ministry of the church and its pastoral vocation. For example, from the age of four to seventeen I felt "called" to play basketball. I had a passion for the game and some gift for the game. I thought the NBA, after a brilliant college career, would be an appropriate place for my athletic gifts. The problem was, I had the gifts to be a high school player and nothing more. I was 5'9", with average speed and a fairly good jump shot. The point is, my gifts did not match my "calling." And the institutional element of the call helped me understand that reality.

The institutional element of the call to ministry involves all the requirements of study, training, preparation, and guidance that leads to ordination. Here, through the frameworks of the church, our understandings of the personal and charismatic elements of our call are tested, guided, and often corrected.

Finally, the democratic element of the call to pastoral ministry is found in the local church that gives us the right and the privilege to serve in a particular time and place. Even in denominational polity arrangements that assure us of a place to minister after we have moved through the other elements of the call process and have been ordained, there is a sense that we can only really minister where we are "invited" to minister.

The first compass (in all of the meanings of the term) that I encourage us to use in our growth toward pastoral clarity, whether we are crossing the bridge from seminary to the parish or are finding our way back to a more focused parish ministry, is to revisit these four aspects of understanding the call. Let's gather our bearings and find true north again in light of these elements of the call. Ask what the stationary point is from which we can pivot and mark off boundaries (or recognize that we really might not have one!). What really is the purview of the pastoral vocation, and does that purview generate a genuine passion within our being? This is what Frederick Buechner means when he speaks of one's vocation being that place where one's deep gladness meets the world's deep need.[1] Finally, what is the compass of our own voice in relationship to these four elements of the call? Who are we, really?! What are our limits within the context of our gifts?

I would suggest using the other compass (in its various meanings), in terms of historical markings, for gaining clarity in the pastoral vocation (and if not clarity, at least personal honesty and integrity), paying careful attention to the vows we will take or have taken at ordination. In many ways, a pastor's word is the only thing a pastor has. What is the word we spoke in our ordination vows? Is our word trustworthy?

What follows is a statement of the basic vows of ordination (or promises made or questions answered) from the ordination services of four major Protestant denominations: Christian Church (Disciples of Christ), United Methodist Church, Presbyterian Church (USA), and Evangelical Lutheran Church in America. Reflect on these vows in light of the four uses of the word compass and see if a kind of clarity begins to form in relationship to:

- getting pastoral bearings and directions,
- finding a pivot point for seeing in all directions and marking off boundaries and limits,
- seeing the purview of the vocation,
- knowing the octaves of one's own voice, one's own self-knowledge.

CHRISTIAN CHURCH (DISCIPLES OF CHRIST)[2]

My sister/brother in the faith, do you believe that you are truly called by God and the Church to the life and work of ministry in the name of Jesus Christ?

Paul the apostle testified, "It is no longer I who live but Christ who lives in me." Will you endeavor to be diligent in your practice of the Christian life: reading the Bible, continuing steadfastly in prayer, and taking up your cross daily to follow Christ?

Scripture teaches that the Church was devoted to the apostles' teaching and fellowship, to the breaking of bread and the prayers. Will you endeavor faithfully to fulfill your calling among the people committed to your care by preaching the word of God and the apostolic faith, and by presiding at the celebration of baptism and the Lord's Supper?

In scripture, ministers are exhorted to tend the flock of God committed to their care, not by constraint but willingly, not for selfish gain but eagerly, not by domineering over those in their charge but by example. Will you endeavor to care for the people of God: nourishing, teaching, and encouraging them; giving direction to the life of the congregation; counseling the troubled; declaring God's forgiveness of sin; and proclaiming victory over death?

The Spirit of God led Jesus to preach good news to the poor, proclaiming release to the captives and recovery of sight to the blind, setting at liberty the oppressed, and proclaiming the time of God's good favor. Will you endeavor to lead the people of God in their obedience to the global mission of the Church: guiding their concern for justice, peace, and freedom for all people; and taking a responsible place in the governance of the Church and in service to the world?

The apostle Paul proclaims the Church to be one body with many members. Will you endeavor to live and work in unity with all Christians: witnessing to the visible unity of the Church; cooperating with Disciples colleagues in the ministry of the congregational, regional, general, and ecumenical church; and leading the Church in fulfilling its ministry of reconciliation?

Paul also wrote, "For me to live is Christ." Will you endeavor to conduct yourself so that your life is shaped by Jesus Christ, who took the form of a servant for our sake; and will you, with the help of the Holy Spirit, continually rekindle the gift of God that is in you, to make known to all people the gospel of the grace of God?

UNITED METHODIST CHURCH[3]

An elder is called to share in the ministry of Christ and of the whole Church: to preach and teach the Word of God and faithfully administer the Sacraments of Holy Baptism and Holy Communion; to lead the people of God in worship and in prayer; to lead persons to faith in Jesus

Christ; to exercise pastoral supervision, order the life of the congregation, counsel the troubled, and declare the forgiveness of sin; to lead the people of God in obedience to mission in the world, to seek justice, peace, and freedom for all people; and to take a responsible place in the government of the Church in service in and to the community. These are the duties of an elder. Do you believe that you are called by God to the life and work of an elder?

PRESBYTERIAN CHURCH (USA)[4]

God has called you by the voice of the church to serve Jesus Christ in a special way. You know who we are and that we serve Jesus Christ in a special way. You know who we are and what we believe, and you understand the work for which you have been chosen. Do you trust in Jesus Christ, your Savior, acknowledge him Lord of all and Head of the Church, and through him believe in one God, Father, Son, and Holy Spirit?

Do you accept the Scriptures of the Old and New Testaments to be, by the Holy Spirit, the unique and authoritative witness to Jesus Christ in the church universal, and God's Word to you?

Do you sincerely receive and adopt the essential tenets of the Reformed faith as expressed in the confession of our church as authentic and reliable expositions of what Scripture leads us to believe and do, and will you be instructed and led by those confessions as you lead the people of God?

Will you be a minister of the Word and Sacrament in obedience to Jesus Christ, under the authority of Scripture, and continually guided by our confessions?

Will you be governed by our church's polity, and will you abide by its discipline? Will you be a friend among your colleagues in ministry, working with them, subject to the ordering of God's Word and Spirit?

Will you in your own life seek to follow the Lord Jesus Christ, love your neighbors, and work for the reconciliation of the world?

Do you promise to further the peace, unity, and purity of the church?

Will you seek to serve the people with energy, intelligence, imagination, and love?

Will you be a faithful minister, proclaiming the good news in Word and Sacrament, teaching faith, and caring for people? Will you be active in government and discipline, serving in the governing bodies of the church; and in your ministry will you try to show the love and justice of Jesus Christ?

EVANGELICAL LUTHERAN CHURCH IN AMERICA[5]

According to apostolic usage you are now to be set apart to the office of Word and Sacrament in the one holy catholic Church by the laying on of hands and by prayer.

Our Lord Jesus Christ says: "Peace be with you. As the Father has sent me, even so I send you. Receive the Holy Spirit. If you forgive the sins of any, they are forgiven; if you retain the sins of any, they are retained."

And again: "All authority in heaven and on earth has been given to me. Go therefore and make disciples of all nations, baptizing them in the name of the Father and of the Son and of the Holy Spirit, teaching them to observe all that I have commanded you; and lo, I am with you always, to the close of the age."

Saint Paul writes: "I received from the Lord what I also delivered to you, that the Lord Jesus on the night when he was betrayed took bread and when he had given thanks, he broke it, and said, 'This is my body which is for you. Do this in remembrance of me.' In the same way also the cup, after supper, saying, 'This cup is the new covenant in my blood. Do this, as often as you drink it, in remembrance of me.' For as often as you eat this bread and drink this cup, you proclaim the Lord's death until he comes."

Before almighty God, to whom you must give account, and in the presence of this congregation, I ask: Will you assume this office, believing that the Church's call is God's call to the ministry of Word and Sacrament?

The Church into which you are to be ordained confesses that the Holy Scriptures are the Word of God and are the norm of its faith and life. We accept, teach, and confess the Apostles', the Nicene, and the Athanasian

Creeds. We also acknowledge the Lutheran Confessions as true witnesses and faithful expositions of the Holy Scriptures. Will you therefore preach and teach in accordance with the Holy Scriptures and these creeds and confessions?

Will you be diligent in your study of the Holy Scriptures and in your use of the means of grace? Will you pray for God's people, nourish them with the Word and Holy Sacraments, and lead them by your own example in faithful service and holy living?

Will you give faithful witness in the world, that God's love may be known in all that you do?

Vows and the Vocation: Common Threads of Clarity

First, faith in Jesus Christ and ministry in his name are reaffirmed as central to ordination promises and to clarity in the pastoral vocation. Various words and phrases are used in the ordination services with regard to this faith in Jesus: apostolic faith, Christ, savior, lord, head, servant. A Trinitarian affirmation is either explicit or implicit in all the ordination services, with reference to God, Jesus, and the Holy Spirit.

Second, the ministry of word and sacrament is the priority in all ordination vows. The focus is on preaching and teaching and administering the sacraments of holy baptism and holy communion. These are defined and expanded in various ways by the traditions. The scriptural emphasis on the church's devotion to the apostles' teaching, fellowship, breaking of bread, and prayers is noted. We must give attention to the apostolic faith, the Bible, the creeds, and the confessions. Reading the Bible and study is central to the vocational task. The overall purpose is to make known the good news and saving grace of the gospel.

Third, tending the people of God is also common to the vows and promises of ordination. This is defined in the various ways of prayer, worship, nurture, counsel, and the proclamation of the forgiveness of sins.

A fourth common thread is attention to the ordering of the life of the church and leading the church to witness in the world through its unity and mission of the peace, love, justice, reconciliation, and freedom of Jesus Christ.

These common threads in the ordination services and vows, along with the four elements of the call to ministry, begin to provide the compasses for the desert journey. Attention to the vows will go a long way toward giving clarity to what the pastor is called to do; such attention will also give clarity to the laity and empower them to be the church in mission and witness to the world. The equation continues to be: pastoral clarity + empowered laity = congregational vitality. We now turn our attention to the difficult task of maintaining the clarity to which the ordination vows point.

CHAPTER 3

Clarity and Ten Theses

In another time of shifting sands and changing paradigms, of pastoral confusion and ecclesial upheaval, the question was asked: Where can I find a Christian holy people? To this question—"What, who, where is the church"—Martin Luther posited seven *notae ecclesiae*.[1] Seven marks identify the church as a place where (1) the word of God is preached; (2) baptism is practiced; (3) the altar is present (holy communion); (4) absolution of sin is experienced; (5) the ordered ministry exists; (6) prayer is faithfully offered; and (7) suffering is shared (the cross). These seven marks of the church provide a quintessential job description for those who are ordained ministers of word and sacrament serving in the local congregation. These marks are indeed a reflection of the common elements of the ordination vows that were explored in the last chapter. What follows are ten theses regarding the pastoral vocation based on these seven marks of the church. These ten theses will lend true clarity to the pastoral vocation in these desert times.[2]

Thesis One

This job description—preaching, baptizing, communing, absolving, praying (publicly and privately), being collegial in ministry, and leaning into pain and suffering—is the focus of the pastoral vocation and does not require other activities or commitments (religious or secular) to demonstrate a pastor's relevance or vindicate a pastor's existence in the church or the world.

Preaching the Word with exegetical, hermeneutical, pastoral, and contextual sensitivity and creativity takes reflective time, creative imagination, and spiritual discernment. Preparing candidates for baptism and their families for this sacrament and the journey it begins involves more than deciding on a time and a date, as if the act were somewhat equivalent to sending out birthday invitations. Making the connections within the life of the parish between the communion table and the common table is essential to mutual ministry between ordained pastors and lay members. It involves preparing the communicants to understand that the bread of both tables, the "daily bread," is tomorrow's bread today, a foretaste of the messianic banquet. It is a matter of deep faith formation. Helping the members of the congregation to grow into the art of spiritual friendship and authentic Christian community at both the communion table in the church and the dinner table in the home, and recognizing them both as "sacramental" and "tables of presence," is a daunting and time-consuming task. To hear confession and offer absolution (a matter we will turn to in part 2 of this book) in any sacramental way involves time, space, and spiritual energy. Developing collegial relationships in the ministry will contribute to a true sense of an "order of ministry." This will challenge the Lone Ranger syndrome so prevalent among Protestant clergy. Commitment to an order of ministry will also take time and focus. Preparing and leading the church toward witness in the world is a daunting task and requires sensitive insights into both the word and the world. Prayer can be neither practiced nor taught in a rushed environment. Being with those who suffer and preparing the congregation to move into places of suffering involves making time to attend to suffering and the discipline of patience. But without attention to human suffering by the church, the mark of the cross is absent from the church. The undergirding of all these tasks of ministry involves prayer, study, reflection, catechesis, visitation, spiritual direction, teaching, solitude, and presence. Talking about the "minister of word and sacrament" is a shorthand way of talking about this job description of the pastoral vocation. It is no abstraction; it is concrete and specific. And it is a full-time job, demanding all a pastor has to give.

Thesis Two

The pastor who is focused on being a minister of word and sacrament will ruthlessly have to say no to the call to many good works and just causes in order to say yes to this call. If one wants to be involved in good works and just causes, in themselves noble callings, one may not be called to the pastoral vocation. The ability to say no to a myriad of voices crying out in need of humanitarian service for the sake of saying yes to the vows taken in ordination is in itself an act of clarification. This is not to denigrate in any way the many critical ways in which care and service need to be rendered in the name of Jesus. But the pastor is trained, prepared, and called to a particular work. The pastor has made promises, and keeping the promises takes all the energy and time available to the pastor. Keeping the promises of the vocation cannot be done faithfully by slipping the pastoral tasks into the cracks in time that would be left between and after "more relevant work."

Thesis Three

This pastoral job description is more than a job, and it is more than a vocation. It is an identity. Becoming clear on the tasks and developing through grace the courage and discipline to attend to them is the working out of the pastor's baptismal identity in Christ. Therefore, the struggle for faithfulness in the pastoral vocation is the pastor's struggle toward Christian discipleship and cross-bearing in the world.

Faithfulness in the vocation is the way the pastor joins the struggle of all the sisters and brothers in the congregation to be faithful to Jesus in the world. A pastor who is faithful to the vocation helps the church to be the church and contributes to the priesthood of all believers. This pastor avoids controlling leadership and lay dependence by empowering the laity to its own leadership, responsibility, and ministry.

One cannot expect the pastoral vocation to be fulfilled except through inward and outward struggle, conflict, and spiritual warfare. Therefore, the pastoral vocation cannot be exercised except by one who struggles continually to live a holy life in daily repentance and simple love of the neighbor. Knowing nothing but "Christ and him crucified," the pastor will expect that most pastoral victories will remain hidden until the day of Jesus Christ. Because of this the pastor is willing to live with the dilemmas and ambiguities that defy easy solution by gimmick or technique. This is one of the connections in a personal way for the pastor between the fifth and seventh of Luther's marks of the church, between the ordered ministry and suffering.[3]

Thesis Four

The pastoral vocation is the vocation to a life of the practice and teaching of prayer. The continual and time-consuming efforts spent in looking for better methods of time management could be better spent in persistent and patient preparation in learning the art of prayer. Nothing is more important to pastoral clarity and ministerial faithfulness than the cultivated and consistent practice of prayer.

In my days as a CPE student chaplain at Columbia Presbyterian Hospital in New York City, I was wrestling with a sense of complete irrelevance working among the highly skilled and technically efficient doctors, nurses, and other assorted medical personnel. I honestly felt out of place, intrusive, and apologetic (not in the sense of "defense") about my presence. I was standing in the emergency room with a woman whose only child had died. "Would you like to pray?" I asked. In great sincerity she quietly answered, "I don't know any prayers." "My God!" I thought, "What has become of prayer?" And with that expletive utterance, I had uttered an honest prayer. It was the beginning for me of a long journey toward trying to learn something of prayer, something of what had become of prayer, and something of the meaning of irrelevance! After all, it was the end of the 1960s, and "irrelevance" was the deadliest of the deadly sins!

The late Henri Nouwen spent the last years of his life being irrelevant and teaching irrelevance. What could be more irrelevant than a brilliant university professor living among mentally handicapped people in a spirit of mutuality? Yet he wrote,

> I am deeply convinced that the Christian leader of the future is called to be completely irrelevant and to stand in this world with nothing to offer but his or her own vulnerable self...The leader of the future will be the one who dares to claim his irrelevance in the contemporary world as a divine vocation that allows him or her to enter into a deep solidarity with the anguish underlying all the glitter of success and to bring the light of Jesus there.[4]

Prayer is, of course, irrelevant. There is so much that cries out to be done. One of the meanings of irrelevant is "not related or pertinent to the matter at hand." It does not mean lack of concern, lack of relationship, or lack of solidarity. In fact, prayer is essentially concern, relationship, and solidarity. But it is not exercised under the tyranny of clamor. It has a different referent point and a different pace and a different focus than immediacy, problem solving, and relevance. Its "home" is in "being" rather than in "accomplishing." And a deep nostalgia for this "home" haunts the lives of so many in the contemporary world who measure identity and worth in little spoonfuls of achievement.

Charles E. Hummel recognizes, even in the world of business, the danger of "the urgent task" that must be done immediately. "The vital task rarely must be done today, or even this week. The urgent task calls for instant action, and in its irresistibility, it devours our energy. But in perspective its deceptive prominence fades. With a sense of loss we recall the vital task we pushed aside. We realize we've become slaves to the tyranny of the urgent."[5] When I reflect on Hummel's statement with pastoral eyes and a pastoral heart, I further recognize what slowly began to dawn on me in the dark hours of the night at Columbia Presbyterian Hospital. The vital task is what has been lost in pastoral ministry for the sake of the urgent task. It is no wonder we suffer pastoral confusion. I know of no place where I or my congregation sees more clearly where Jesus would have us be than in the place of intercessory prayer and contemplative prayer. When pastors "close their eyes" in prayer, their vision will be clarified and their vocation focused.

When they teach their congregations to pray, when they call the congregation to public prayer, the vision and vocation of the church will be clarified.

"My God! What has become of prayer?" Perhaps we pastors have hidden it because we feared irrelevancy! The disciples came to Jesus and asked, "Lord, teach us to pray." I believe that is the vital task of the pastoral vocation and the request even our congregations are afraid to voice.

Thesis Five

The phrase "minister of the word" used in the ordination service is no abstraction. It is an accurate summary term for the pastoral vocation. It signifies that the pastoral vocation requires one to spend much prayerful time with the Bible. The pastor who is no longer studying, praying over, learning, and teaching the scriptures has abandoned the holy ministry. This pastor may be very busy, but without the centering of the "ministry of the word" in the Word, there can be no clarity for the vocation of the Word.

One of the difficulties for today's desert pastor, however, is that words themselves have become cheap, misused, and abused in almost every sphere of life. They are often no longer used to convey truth or meaning or beauty. Quite the opposite is true in many ways. They are used to lie, obfuscate, and injure. We have come to accept this as a matter of course in the realms of politics and advertising. But it is also true of common usage in day-to-day conversation. And, sadly, it is true in the sphere of religious discourse. So much religious language is overblown hyperbole that it becomes extremely difficult to say yes or no, or to speak with care, truthfulness, and humility in addressing the mysteries of our humanity within the life of God.

Rabbi Abraham Heschel gave much of his life to raising the issue of "holiness in words."

> The renewal of man involves a renewal of language. To the man of our age, nothing is as familiar and trite as words. Of all things they are the cheapest, most abused, and least esteemed. They are the objects of perpetual defilement. We all live in them, but since we fail to uphold their independent dignity, they turn waif, elusive, a mouthful of dust. When placed before the Bible, the words of which are like dwellings made of rock, we do not know how to find the door. There is no understanding of the God of Israel without deep sensitivity to the holiness in words. For what is the Bible? Holiness in words. And we destroy all the gates of the Bible by the ongoing desecration of the power of the word...Promiscuity of expression, loss of sensitivity to words, has nearly destroyed the fortress of the spirit. And the fortress of the spirit is the *debar,* the word. Words have become slums. What we need is a renewal of words.[6]

One of the difficulties for pastors and churches today is that we have lost faith in words and placed our faith in direct action.

The pastor is one who loves and serves and reverences human language. The minister of the word recognizes the power of words to create worlds, heal, injure, lift up, and bring down. From this reverence for human language and respect for the power of words, the minister of the word recognizes and honors language as the covenanted medium of the Holy Spirit's saving and sanctifying work. The faithful reading of the Bible as a pastor will naturally entail the reading of theology, creeds, confessions, and histories of interpretation. It will also involve what I have already called the ability to read "worlds" through familiarity with literature, biography, psychology, sociology, and history. Simply put, the pastoral vocation is a vocation in words and the Word.

Of course, the word one speaks is the word one hears. In the Revelation to John, the importance of the word and the scroll and what is written and what is spoken is a powerful theme from the opening verses to the closing verses. "Blessed is the one who reads...the words...and blessed are those who hear." Each of the seven letters to the seven churches begins: "These are the words of him who..." It is the word that is "eaten." It is significant that the one who experiences this vision is told not to "open the scroll" or "scan the word" but to "eat the word" and that it would lie sour in the belly but sweet on the tongue (Rev. 10:9–10). Many pastors today fear the eating of the word because of the heaviness in the belly, and our stomachs usually know when to turn before our minds do! But as a disciple of Jesus, who works out that discipleship in the pastoral vocation, the pastor is called to listen to the words of scripture as an address of God's Word to his or her own life and the life of the parish that is served.

Thesis Six

Because the pastoral vocation centers in word, sacrament, and prayer, the pastor's weekly path leads to and from the public liturgy— the work of the people of God. "Liturgy *(leitourgia)* is the public work performed by a particular community under the leadership of its liturgists *(leitourgoi)* to enact its view of reality and commitments."[7] Here the church is created by the Holy Spirit. It will, therefore, serve the pastor's vocational clarity if not too much time passes between the public gatherings of the congregation for worship.

Seven days is too long a gap between public gatherings for worship. Condensing the worship life of the congregation to an hour a week out of the 168 hours available represents a clear sellout to the culture. The practice and experience of Sabbath rest has nearly disappeared from our spiritual life together. The heartbeat of parish life sounds from the chancel rather than the church office, the boardroom, and sites of committee meetings. A pastor who is calling laity from their busy daily lives to committee meetings, workshops, house cleanings, and work sessions more often than to prayer and worship is serving the present confusion about the true nature and identity of God's ecclesia in the world.

More times of prayer, study, and meditation; expanded opportunities of worship; and calling the faithful into sacred space for sacred time in sacred togetherness will help lead the church into its true vocation. In a time when people are in flight from reality through the frenzied pursuit of fantasy, a flight ultimately from the experience of God and the presence of God as well as the experience and recognition of their true humanity, the pastor's task is to hold a place open for God. In a time when the principalities and powers demand unconditional allegiance, the most radical act available to the Christian congregation through the pastoral leadership of the minister is worship. For here the community of faith enacts its view of reality, renews its commitments, clarifies its identity, and celebrates its faith before God and the world. As William Temple put it, "To worship is to quicken the conscience by the holiness of God, to feed the mind by the truth of God, to purge the imagination by the beauty of God and to open the heart to the love of God."[8]

Thesis Seven

The vocational clarity of pastors will be greatly served by a true *ministerium* (the fifth *notae* in Luther's "marks"), the ordered ministry. Pastors need to recognize that we have entered an "order of ministry." We are not simply freelance entrepreneurs in the church of God. The tendency toward Lone Rangerism and the temptation to isolationism is great. This is partially the case because no intentional effort is made at judicatory or regional levels to make the current gatherings of ministerial colleagues into an authentic *ministerium*. Such meetings are often reduced to chit chat, reportage, and institutional and organizational matters. They become such a bore that it is no wonder pastors begin to think they are a waste of time.

A true *ministerium* is an honest fellowship in the gospel. It is a fellowship in the word of God and in prayer. Such a *ministerium* would involve mutual confession and absolution; times of study, prayer, and meditation; and a systematic focusing of pastoral attention on theological reflection on the practice of ministry. A systematic schedule of mutual pastoral visitation with other pastors in their own parish settings for the purpose of encouragement and pastoral accountability should be welcomed. This practice would mitigate against the loneliness of the vocation and would enhance the understanding of belonging to an order of holy ministry. It would also contribute to the practice of discernment and would build collegial relationships in such a way as to create genuine living connections and appreciations beyond the parameters of the local congregation.

Thesis Eight

The pastor's vocational clarity is marked by a true sense of the mediation of the word of God in relationship to the congregation and all individual members in the congregation in every circumstance. This discipline of spiritual relationships is essential to the exercise of the pastoral office and the maintenance of integrity between the pastor and the people.

How is the pastor related to each member of the congregation? The great temptation for many pastors is to relate directly and emotionally through the power and influence of the pastor's personality. It is in this area that we enter the difficult and thorny issues of the pastor's personhood, the pastor's humanity, the pastor's own needs. Here we are confronted with the question of intimacy and distance, of boundaries and thresholds, in relationships that inevitably involve vulnerability, attention, passion, love, care, and need (those characteristics at the heart of the gospel).

The current approach to this question, when it is addressed at all, usually falls into two categories. One, while not overtly stated, is the practice of ministry as the cult of personality. The other, advocated in many workshops on pastoral ethics, is the attempt to eliminate any kind of friendship within the congregation. This seems ironic to me in that Jesus referred to his incipient community as friends. I believe neither of these approaches to be either theologically sound or pastorally advisable. If the pastor's own vulnerability is the human ground out of which he or she offers ministry, and if the graces of the gospel are to be incarnate and relational in the community, then the nature of the pastor's congregational relationships should be neither superficially distant, artificial, or condescending, nor manipulative, charming, or personality focused.

The pastor should live in both "holy distance" and "holy intimacy" with all members of the parish. The discernment of both the distance and the intimacy is a matter of spiritual discipline in which the pastor recognizes the space—whether distance or intimacy—as the space in which Christ stands. This is, in one sense, liturgical space, and the distance and intimacy are served by the right distinction between the office of ministry and the person in ministry.

One of the reasons for the power and place of clerical dress and vestments is to mark this distinction between office and person visibly and concretely. This holy distance is not for the sake of elevating the pastor's person or for holding the pastor aloof from others. It is for the sake of the true service to the Word and the true intimacy of the fellowship of the Word.

The disciplined practice of holy distance is especially urgent in relations with those to whom the pastor is, humanly speaking, socially or emotionally close: our families and our friends. In the order of creation it is right and natural that there are those to whom the pastor is closer than others. Since the Christian congregation lives in the world and not in heaven, this will be true also within the congregation. But in the order of redemption, the pastor lives equidistant from every member of the Christian community. And the pastor's relationships with them are in, through, and for the sake of Christ.

This discipline of Christian relationships must govern all expectations of the pastor toward the congregation and the congregation toward the pastor. It should be a matter of teaching and open conversation within parish life. As Bonhoeffer demonstrated in *Life Together,* this is simply the communal implication of the doctrine of justification by grace through faith. Our identity, both individually and communally, as pastor and parishioner, is the work of the word of God *extra nos,* to be received in faith.

Thesis Nine

The vocational clarity of the pastor is not simply for the good of the pastor; it is for the good of the whole people of God. Clarity begets clarity. I mentioned earlier in this book the vicious cycle of our current situation: If the church is unclear regarding its identity and mission, how can the pastor know what he or she is being called to be and do; if the pastor is unclear regarding the pastoral vocation, how can the church ever discover its identity and mission? The pastor's clarity about the vocation, about the distinct way of pastoral discipleship in the world, will serve the vocational clarity of laity in their priestly work in the world and their discipleship and crossbearing. It will free and empower them to assume their roles and responsibilities in being the church. Clear about the nature and limitations of the pastoral calling, the pastor can see the urgency of lay discipleship and ministry in the world. From the dignity of the pastor's own calling, the pastor can honor and teach the dignity of the calling and duties of the lay ministry.

Thesis Ten

The clarity of the pastoral vocation and pastoral identity turns out to be a matter not primarily of time management, administrative brilliance, professionalism, technique, and more self-discipline, but a matter of faith in Jesus Christ.

To refuse to rest and work within the limitations of the call to be a public minister of word and sacrament is to doubt the promise of Jesus Christ in baptism and ordination! To doubt the personal, communal, political, and social efficacy of the publicly preached Word and the faithfully celebrated sacraments, to doubt the efficacy of the church's liturgy, and so to seek relevance or fulfillment or justification in and by some other work, is to disobey Jesus and to doubt his promises! To abandon the therapy of the word of God for simple human therapies and clever manipulative techniques is to abandon faith in Jesus Christ! To doubt that the words of scripture address God's Word most directly to one's own life and the life of the congregation one serves, and so to abandon patient prayerful meditation on the Word and prayerful existence on behalf of the world and the people of God in search of some spiritual secret of pastoral success and effectiveness, represents a loss of faith in Jesus!

Such is my understanding of the critical nature of pastoral vocational clarity for the church catholic and confessing in this new century, in this desert time. Without such clarity on the part of the church and its pastors, we will end up with a church with no identity, indistinguishable from the myriad cultural voices that call to us today in the larger world. The gospel itself is endangered when those called to the ministry of word and sacrament forget their vocational focus. For without this kerygmatic and sacramental focus, the historical memory of the church, and, by extension, the gospel, is under threat.

It is to the working out of these theses in specific and concrete terms in the life of the pastor and the pastor's daily and weekly relationship with the congregation that we now turn.

CHAPTER 4

Creativity: Images and Imagination

To this point we have been focused on the need for pastoral vocational clarity. We have considered current confusions, inadequate reactions, ordination promises, and historic connections. Desert travel also calls for creativity. Connectedness to historical functions and ordination promises, to focus and clarity, does not mean the foregoing of creativity in the practice of ministry.

The desert experience has led to the death of creative imagination within the pastoral vocation and the life of the church. Usually pastors know how important it is to develop vision, mission, and values within a congregation. All of these are critically important, but there is another issue that needs to be addressed prior to the work required on these elements. What will give dynamism to vision making, mission statements, and values clarifications is the rebirth of images and imagination within the congregation. To move to vision, mission, and values without the undergirding imaginative images that are developed, understood, and shared communally is to make the former seem to be daunting burdens and justification by works.

Vision making concerns itself with the kind of world the pastor and the congregation want to create together with God. Mission statements express the specific ways in which the community goes about creating the vision in its own limited and specific context. Values are those mutually agreed-on ways in which people want to be together as community in pursuit of the vision through the specific mission. But before all of this should come the creative and imaginative task of developing the images that inform and inspire the pastor and the people together. Image making is a communal task. What is the primary image of the pastor? What is the primary image the congregation holds of itself? Has a guiding and informing and inspiring image ever been articulated? Are the images that lie below the surface of the collective consciousness of the congregation accurate or truthful?

It is ineffective and counterproductive for the pastor to develop his or her own image of the church and then to attempt to impose it on the congregation. Malaise, a current problem within many congregations, is related to the absence of any coherent or compelling image for the church and the pastor. Malaise is an indefinite feeling of debility or lack of health often indicative of or accompanying the onset of an illness. It is the vague feeling of mental, emotional, moral, or spiritual ill-being. Communally, it will lead to disillusionment, disappointment, lack of enthusiasm, lack of interest, lack of vitality, and lack of identity. It will express itself through lack of commitment, participation, and growth. If congregational revitalization is to occur and a spiritual vision for the church is to be developed, the exercise of creative imagination and the discovery and adoption of realistic communal images is crucial. This applies to both the image of the pastor and the image of the congregation.

Paul Minear's work remains among the most helpful resources for understanding the role of imagination and images within the Christian congregation.[1]

> Images serve as a mode for perceiving a given reality, especially where this reality is of such a nature as not to be amenable to objective visibility or measurement. Any reality that is inherently a mystery will demand for its perception the awakening of the imagination. So will any reality whose existence is a sign, however ambiguous, of the operation of the invisible demonic or divine forces. The same is true of those realities which are of such proportions as to extend beyond the range of human manipulation or organization.[2]

The realities of the spiritual life—the Christian mission, the community of faith, the work of the Holy Spirit, the nature of the sacramental, the realm of mystery—lie beyond the reach of manipulation and technique. They lie not only within but beyond the realm of discursive language. Their perception requires more than explanation. The method of "knowing" in the West has been reduced in many ways to observation and description, followed by explanation. To a great extent we have become slaves to the scientific paradigm and have lost the capacity to reject its idolatry. Participation in divine/human realities and the dimension of the sacramental understanding of life require creative imagination. I do not mean by this a return to magic, but I do mean a reopening of the place of mystery for the understanding of human existence at its depths and an expansion in our ways of knowing. What, then, is the difference between fantasy and imagination? Fantasy fails to live in the world of facts, truths, and realities. Imagination, on the other hand, is not divorced from facts, truths, and realities, but is a way of illumination.

Minear goes on to say,

> Every person carries about with him a gallery of self images...Once he believes firmly that a picture is right for him, he will shape his emotions and actions accordingly. And much will depend on whether the picture is authentic, and dependably so. The same principle applies to any primary community. Its self-understanding, its inner cohesion, its *espirit de corps*, derive from a dominant image of itself, even though that image remains inarticulately imbedded in subconscious strata. If an unauthentic image dominates its consciousness, there will first be subtle signs of malaise, followed by more overt tokens of communal deterioration...The process of discovering and rediscovering an authentic self-image will involve the whole community not only in clearheaded conceptual thinking and disciplined speech, but also in a rebirth of its images and its imagination, and in the absorption of these images into the interstices of communal activities of every sort.[3]

This description of the role of images and imagination not only in personal identity but in communal life illustrates some of the reasons for malaise in our current desert existence. The description also points to why pastors and congregations should begin by imaginatively focusing on images prior to addressing concerns with vision making, mission statements, and values formation.

Finally, Minear points out that

> our self-understanding is never complete, never uncorrupted, never deep enough, never wholly transparent.

In every generation the use and re-use of the biblical images has been one path by which the church has tried to learn what the church truly is, so that it could become what it is not. For evoking this kind of self-knowledge, images may be more effective than formal dogmatic assertions. This may well be one reason why the New Testament did not legislate any particular definition of the church and why Christian theology has never agreed upon any such definition.[4]

In this desert time of lack of pastoral vocational clarity and ecclesial confusion, nothing may be more important than the mutual recovery of authentic ministerial and congregational images. This may well be the single most significant desert path to be taken in order to learn what the church truly is so that it can become what it is not, but needs to be.

It is vital that the pastor's self-image be shared with and understood by the congregation. Otherwise, confusion regarding the pastor's way of being and tasks performed within the congregation will be rampant. It is equally important for the congregation and the pastor to engage together in the mutual exploration, development, and adoption of the congregation's image of the church. Finally, it is essential that the pastor's self-image and the congregation's controlling images of the church be in coherence with each other. If they are not, the result will likely be confusion, conflict, and malaise.

Pastoral Images

Pastoral images are not the same as the job description of pastors discussed in the last chapter. The job description is the essentiality of the vocation. Images are powerful means by which the pastor and the congregation find common understanding, shared power, mutual appreciation, imaginative guidance, and inspiration for fulfilling the job description within the parish.

A number of pastoral theologians have offered various images of the pastoral vocation. Urban T. Holmes has suggested such images as the mana/manna person ("mana" in Jungian terms of being related to the sacral or the divine, and "manna" in terms of the bringer of bread); clown (the desacralizer of untruths and false pretensions; it has been said that there are two intellectuals in society—the clown and the priest. The clown makes us laugh at what we think about, and the priest makes us think about what we laugh at); storyteller (the human and divine stories and their intersection); wagon master (following the imagery of wilderness and journey).[5] Eugene Peterson has suggested the images of the unbusy pastor, the subversive pastor, and the apocalyptic pastor.[6]

Letty Russell has used pastoral images related to table fellowship.[7] Donald Messer has explored such images as political mystics in a prophetic community, enslaved liberators of the rainbow church, and practical theologians in a postdenominational church.[8] Henri Nouwen has advocated images of movement: from relevance to prayer, from popularity to ministry, from leading to being led.[9]

All of these images are fruitful and suggestive; none of them are complete or exhaustive, nor do these writers intend them to be. Three things are important as the pastor works toward pastoral vocational clarity and imaginative expressions of that pastoral identity: (1) The image must be authentic to the pastor's own personhood; (2) it must be able to contain and contribute to the vocational job description; and (3) it must be openly shared and reflected on with the congregation that one serves.

Congregational Images

Congregational images are not the same as definitions of the church or mission statements. They are an imaginative way of expressing the nature of the essential togetherness and identity and mission of the specific community in a specific context in a specific moment of history. This is one of the reasons images become ineffective and unarticulated—communities change, contexts alter, moments of historical circumstance fluctuate. Often congregations hold on to subconscious (or conscious) images that are no longer accurate or meaningful. Reimaging is a repeated theological exercise within the congregation.

Background help in exploring congregational images can be found in the work of Paul Minear,[10] Avery Dulles,[11] Sallie McFague,[12] and Letty Russell,[13] and in my own work.[14] Again, none of these images is exhaustive. There is much creative work to be done in terms of contemporary and contextual images, and it must be done by pastors and local congregations.

Three things are important in the development of congregational images of the church: (1) They must be expressive of the church catholic and confessing in terms of the historical tradition; (2) they must be truthful and authentic to the actual life of the congregation as it exists or is seeking intentionally to become;

and (3) they must be arrived at through the community's mutual theological reflection and be readily available in terms of understanding, inspiration, identity formation, expression, and contributing to a creative *espirit de corps.*

The role of imagination is important in other areas besides the development of pastoral vocational images and congregational identity images. One of those areas is the way we come to speak our faith in the desert. I have argued that the pastoral vocation is a "way of speaking." This is, of course, true of the Christian life and the life of the Christian community as a whole. The Christian faith is a faith in the "word made flesh." We speak through preaching, teaching, confessing, ritual, pastoral care, evangelism, dialogue, encouraging. But what if we as pastors, and by extension our congregations, have forgotten how to "speak Christian"? Our culture and our churches certainly know how to speak TV, speak sports, speak advertising, speak consumerism, speak greed, speak patriotism, speak scientifically. Do we know how to speak Christian?

The mode for speaking Christian involves sacred story, parables, poetry, liturgical actions, and silence. These modes of speaking belong to the world of enchantment. Enchantment comes to us in English from *in contare*: to sing! From that word we get cantor and chant. To enchant means to influence by charm, to attract, to rouse, to bewitch, to move deeply. Other words for enchant are enthrall, spellbind, gratify, delight, and enrapture. I wonder when the last time was that we simply fell to our knees, enthralled with the wonder of it all. I wonder when we have, as pastors, enraptured people with the faith rather than simply studied the faith or explained the faith. Vital religion is not simply believed, it is danced. Vital congregations dance their faith. The dances of faith may be mournful or joyful, but they are nonetheless dances. For this reason it is important to recover the whole concept of enchantment in how we speak Christian to our children, to our young people, to our elderly, and to our rational selves. I have some sense of loss as both a theologian and a pastor for reducing "knowing" to "reasoning." I have opted for rational thought because I fear irrationality (and not without cause!). I am not arguing, as the old saying goes, that we should leave our brains at the door of the church. But neither should we leave our "selves," our whole selves, at the door of the church. We do this when we reduce Christian knowing to rational thought. It is, to be sure, a reductionism.

Enchantment is wonder, and wonder is a very important part of faith. Faith is not simply about facts and information. To speak in wonder, to speak in enchantment, to speak Christian, is more like saying "I do" at a wedding than it is to expound or explain. It is the giving of oneself in a relationship.

Speaking Christian, like the first speaking of God, is to create. It is to create a world. Karl Marx had it right in one sense: The purpose of philosophy is not to explain the world but to change it. To speak Christian with imagination and wonder and enchantment is to create a new world for new people. It is to sing a new world and new possibilities into being. It is to say no to the world as it is in favor of the world as it might be in the deepest desires of a spiritually refined heart.

To believe that the world is only as you currently see it or think it is, is extremely limiting. The world is a mysterious place. The desert is a mysterious place. Think of the times you have looked out over a vista, whether landscape or cityscape, after the sun has just risen and the dew still clings to the face of the earth. Or in the twilight, the dying light of a long-spent day. Or after a thundershower. You see the world a little differently in the dawn, the sunset, and the thundershower's aftermath. The world is seen from a slant.

To speak Christian is to help people see the world differently, to enter into a different world. The great children's stories do this: C. S. Lewis's *The Chronicles of Narnia*, J. R. R. Tolkien's *The Hobbit*, Lewis Caroll's *Alice's Adventures in Wonderland*, and even J. K. Rowling's Harry Potter series. All these create worlds of enchantment. And so does the Bible, in the creative imagination of a deft interpreter who has learned how to speak Christian. When we are dealing with God, prayer, worship, redemption, sacrament, presence, mystery, and spirituality, we are desperately in need of the language of imagination and enchantment. Creating the world of enchantment, of course, is not all up to the pastor. The congregation must also be a community of interpretation. The experiences, creativity, and poetic and imaginative insights of the whole community contribute to the process.

Urban Holmes has spoken of Jesus as the "imaginative shock" to his culture.[15] Marcus Borg, building on the work of Huston Smith, pursues the importance of "root images" in addressing and understanding reality.[16] Ministers of word and sacrament who have begun to operate out of vocational clarity soaked in the historic traditions and authentic pastoral images honed in creative imagination can begin to bring an imaginative shock to our culture and our churches. Think of the history of biblical and Christian faith. Sarah's story is a story of imaginative shock at the news of her pregnancy. Nathan was the imaginative shock to King David in his simple parable. All of the prophets were imaginative shocks to their culture and the enculturated communities of faith where they spoke and acted out their ministries. Mary the virgin is a story of imaginative shock at the annunciation. Paul received an imaginative shock on the road to Damascus and became an imaginative shock to an exclusivist church. Augustine, after years of debauchery, experienced an imaginative shock in the garden in Milan and became an imaginative shock to a church and an empire during the empire's decline. Martin Luther was an imaginative shock to an awakening Europe. Rosa Parks used her weariness, not just from a day's work but from her life's experience, to be an imaginative shock to a bus driver, a city, and a nation. Martin Luther King, Jr., "dreamed a dream" and was an imaginative shock to a particular people and an entire nation. Mother Teresa was an imaginative shock to a church and a world that does its best to forget the least and the last.

All these people created new worlds of possibility, and people were enchanted. How can ministers of word and sacrament read these texts with passionless "ho-humness" and convey them to congregations in such ways that preaching is in danger of becoming the euthanasia of people's faith? Perhaps we have forgotten how to speak Christian in terms of sacred story, parable, poetry, liturgical actions, and silence.

Malcolm Muggeridge, curmudgeon that he was, knew something of this dimension of the faith experience, perhaps because he fought with it most of his life and came to it late in his life. He used to spend a good deal of time at the British Museum in the illuminated manuscript room. Stored and displayed here were the ancient manuscripts that had been adorned, illustrated, gold leafed, and "illuminated" in beautiful and profound artistic expression. These manuscripts were enchanting. Muggeridge spoke of being in this room as "being in the illuminated." It became a metaphor for him of becoming and living as a Christian. Speaking Christian with creative imagination is the process of illuminating the world by the light that has shined and has not been overcome by darkness.

CHAPTER 5

Confessions and Theological Foundations

Any understanding of pastoral identity and the pastoral vocation is ultimately rooted in one's understanding of the nature of the God who calls one to ministry. In ministry, a person responds to a prior call rather than simply choosing a profession. One enters a vocation rather than a career. Of course, it is possible, if one sees ministry as a career, not to let any understanding of God interfere with the progress of the career! Therefore, the struggle to develop and maintain vocational integrity begins the first day of one's ministry and will last a lifetime. But the choice remains between "vocational holiness and career idolatry."[1] If the ministry is theocentric vocation rather than career humanitarianism, one's understanding of the nature of God is crucial, for it will shape one's understanding and practice of ministry. The God one confesses fashions the ministry one practices. One's ministry and vocational identity must be rooted in theology, for ministry itself is concerned with life that flows from God, in God, to God.

The Knowledge of God

The knowledge of God in Hebrew thought (*da'ath elohim*) is passionate relationship rather than facts and information. Ministry should be grounded in this Hebrew perspective rather than the Greek philosophical categories of omnipotence, omniscience, omnipresence, immutability, and impassibility. These Greek views do not come from biblical confessional narratives concerning God.

This is not just esoteric, abstract, philosophical speculation. Warped theology has warped consequences. Therefore, careful attention must be paid to the theological foundations of the pastoral vocation.

These Greek conceptions have been pervasive in Western thought and theology and have greatly influenced the faith and practice of not only the church in general but clerical abuses in particular. They have greatly influenced the church's self-understanding, its understanding of power and authority, and its way of being in the world. A few examples will suffice to illustrate the point.

If the God we confess is omnipotent, we are reduced to worshiping "god almightiness." We may desire almightiness in order to be "like" God. This affects the way the church and its clergy understand power and why the church has historically so often gone whoring after power. If the God we confess is immutable, this affects the church's attitude toward change. Certitude, absolutism, and changelessness become high values. If the God we confess is impassible or passionless, we may crave invulnerability and security above all else. The church does not baptize in the name of the omnipotent, the immutable, and the impassible. It baptizes in the name of the triune God whose narrative name in the Bible is Father, Son, and Holy Spirit.

The doctrine of the Trinity points to the nature of God as being social, relational, and communal in essence. The power of God in its very nature is shared power. It also points to the nature of God as being a dynamic and differentiated reality, which makes possible the confession of the power of God as being self-giving love. This is the deepest meaning of God's being-in-relationship. God is not the will-to-power but the will-to-community in love, freedom, and justice. God's power and authority are defined not by limitlessness but by God's nature.

If the God who calls a person into ministry and the church into existence is not a God who is sheer power (or god almightiness), this can lead to the self-limiting use of power by both the clergy and the church. It will be a shared power for the sake of community in love, freedom, and justice. If this God is relational in nature, the clergy and the church can exercise other-affirming power. Finally, if this God continues to seek relationship for the sake of a yet incomplete future, the clergy and the church can exercise future-opening power in places and among persons where the future is closed because of the lack of love, freedom, and justice in community. In short, the theological foundations of the ministry are in the nature of the God who calls to ministry. The God of the Hebrew and Christian traditions is a God of self-limiting, other-affirming, future-opening power.[2] In understanding that the God who calls to ministry and to the community of love, freedom, and justice is not just sheer power, the church and its clergy can begin to reflect creatively on the nature of authority and empowerment in determining its identity, authenticity, life together, and mission.

The abuse of power, the pride and inflexibility of certitude and absolutism, and the hard protective shell of invulnerability are signs, not of life, but of death. They are the enemies of pastoral clarity and ministerial authenticity, barriers to genuinely relational community in the church, and stumbling blocks to the church's witness in the world. They are "theological sins" because they arise out of a false view of God and God's power. It is, therefore, at the point of the theological foundations of pastoral ministry that these enemies must be addressed and the pastoral vocation clarified.

The failure to come to grips with this understanding of the nature of God's power has had a terrible trickle-down effect on the whole life of the church and the exercise of the pastoral ministry within it. Carlyle Marney has stated this effect very clearly:

> When we separated power from love and justice and opted for power, we came up with a fatal-to-the-gospel series of substitutes: clergy for laity, rank for brotherhood, learning for devotement, function over relation, prestige for integrity, institution for fellowship, committees instead of service, property for community, and ritual in place of liturgy. In short, we turned from communion, work-service, and the free dance around a proper altar which is worship *(koinonia, diakonia,* and *leiturgia)*—all in the name of organized service to God.[3]

The recovery of pastoral clarity will be greatly enhanced by more careful attention to the nature of the God who calls to ministry. The vocation itself will be rooted in passionate relationship, exercised by the use of self-giving love; restrained by self-limiting, other-affirming, future-opening power; and directed by a will-to-community in love, freedom, and justice.

Tucked away in the little and often overlooked book of Habakkuk is an insight of crucial importance in coming to terms with pastoral vocational clarity in relationship to the nature of the God who calls to ministry. This insight reveals the constant danger and threat of idolatrous power to vocational clarity. "What use is an idol once its maker has shaped it—a cast image, a teacher of lies?...Alas for you who say to the wood, 'Wake up!' to silent stone, 'Rouse yourself!' Can it teach? See, it is gold and silver plated, and there is no breath in it at all. But the LORD is in God's holy temple; let all the earth keep silence before God!"[4] Three series of questions emerge from this text relating to clarity in the pastoral vocation and the nature of the church's life and ministry in the world.

Is the pastoral ministry, in solidarity with the whole ministry of the Christian congregation, going about the business of revelation? Is this partnership in the gospel, marked by being a hearing and responding and interpretive community, providing a locus and environment for divine epiphany and holy presence? Is the Christian community, with the guidance of its minister of word and sacrament, actually "holding the world open for God?" Is the church a sanctuary for the meeting place between God and God's people where revelation can actually occur? Is the pastoral ministry functioning in such a way within the fellowship-service-worship community of faith as to be a place of meaning making? Put another way, in this desert experience, can the church and its pastoral ministry interpret existence toward meaning through the lens of the gospel of Jesus Christ, or has it chased after idols that were never meant to be and cannot be the source of its life?

In addition to creating a locus and environment conducive to divine revelation and meaning making, is the pastoral ministry and the church a source for "breath"? In other words, is the church and its ministry about life? Does the ministry engender life and make life possible? The centering theological question for the desert experience, and therefore the theological foundational question for vocational clarity in the ministry of word and sacrament, is: What is the word that gives life?

In the fractured busyness of pastoral life and the resulting confusion that is present in vocational consciousness, is the minister of word and sacrament attending to silence, that mode of being out of which authentic Christian speaking arises? Is there ever present in the consciousness of the pastor and the church the command of Jesus to the demons: "Be silent!"? Is there an intentional time and place of silence within the life of the pastor and the functioning of the church where a transcendent voice might be heard and awe and reverence again experienced before the life-engendering presence of God? The difference between God and the idolatrous manifestation of power and authority is the power to engender life. In the idol there is no breath, there is no spirit life! The focused pastoral vocation is a constant struggle against all pernicious forms of idolatry, personal and communal. Indeed, what is the word that gives life? Is there enough silence in the midst of the idolatrous clamor of present-day ministry to hear that word and then to speak it?

Biblical Images and Narratives

The theological foundations of pastoral vocational clarity evolve, however, not only from the way we confess God and the nature of God's power. They evolve from the images, narratives, and metaphors that inform the implementation of self-giving love and the expression of self-limiting, other-affirming, future-opening power. There are, of course, many images, narratives, and metaphors that can prove helpful, but we initially stray from the biblical ones to our peril. Since we are looking for informative images and metaphors for clarity as ministers of word and sacrament, I have chosen texts from the variety of canonical literature out of which pastors work and that are read liturgically from the balanced guidance given us in the common lectionary: Torah, prophets, epistles, gospel. My intention in offering these texts is not to be exhaustive in scope, content, or comment, but to be suggestive for the exercise of pastoral creative imagination.

The text from the Torah is Exodus 3:1–12; 4:10–12, the call of Moses. This narrative is a reminder that it is God who calls and God who accomplishes. Somehow, somewhere, in that way that is beyond all human comprehension, the bush has burned for pastors and we have heard the call to ministry. "Take off your shoes." And know this: We stand on holy ground; for ministry, like the God who calls to ministry, is grounded in holiness. And as with Moses, it is God who takes the stammering of one's life and gives the gift of ministry. Paul provides an appropriate commentary here. The treasure is not the container. Rather, "we have this treasure in clay jars, so that it may be made clear that this extraordinary power belongs to God and does not come from us...Not that we are competent of ourselves to claim anything as coming from us; our competence is from God, who has made us competent to be ministers of a new covenant."[5] Remember always that ministry is a holiness and a gift. It is God who calls and God who accomplishes, and we, by grace, have an opportunity to be God's vessels in the sacrament of ministry.

Two texts from the prophets are suggestive pointers to the theological foundations of the ministry of word and sacrament. The first is Isaiah 58:6–11.

> Is not this the fast that I choose: to loose the bonds of injustice, to undo the thongs of the yoke, to let the oppressed go free, and to break every yoke? Is it not to share your bread with the hungry, and bring the homeless poor into your house; when you see the naked, to cover them, and not to hide yourself from your own kin? Then your light shall break forth like the dawn, and your healing shall spring up quickly; your vindicator shall go before you, the glory of the LORD shall be your rear guard. Then you shall call, and the LORD will answer; you shall cry for help, and God will say, Here I am. If you remove the yoke from among you, the pointing of the finger, the speaking of evil, if you offer your food to the hungry and satisfy the needs of the afflicted, then your light shall rise in the darkness and your gloom be like the noonday. The LORD will guide you continually, and satisfy your needs in parched places, and make your bones strong; and you shall be like a watered garden, like a spring of water, whose waters never fail.

This "parched places" text is appropriate to the context of our desert experience in the pastoral vocation. This text from Isaiah is three chapters prior to the text Jesus chose to begin his ministry with in Nazareth,[6] and it reflects the same themes. When Jesus spoke of the text as being fulfilled, he promptly began preaching and teaching, healing and exorcizing, and calling together a community of compassion in which the marginalized were welcomed and the suffering were attended to. The pastoral vocation is one that lifts up in the compassionate community the plight of human need and the call to human care. The "voice" of the pastoral vocation is the voice of the poor, the oppressed, the outsider, and the forgotten. It is Christian speaking on their behalf to the community of compassion. This is the task of the minister of word and sacrament—to be the voice of the voiceless.

The text also is a reminder that ministry is composed of both fast days and feast days. There is a rhythm in pastoral ministry of solitude and community, of fasting and feasting, of service and celebration. There is a sharing in the pain and a rejoicing at the party. We fast alone; we feast together. If one pours oneself out for the hungry and satisfies the needs of the afflicted (calling the people of God to this kind of fast), God's light will shine through one's ministry. The feast days will come.

The metaphor of the well-watered garden is then introduced by the prophet and becomes a powerful image of ministry as oasis in these desert times. Attention to the theological foundations of pastoral ministry will surely contribute to being "like a spring...whose waters never fail." The living out of vocational faithfulness by its pastors will provide the church access to that deep underground spring from which faith is watered and the Christian life is nurtured and sustained. It will provide access to the healing fountains.

The second text from the prophets that informs pastoral clarity in the pastoral vocation is Ezekiel 34:1–16. This text is an indictment of the lack of vocational clarity and integrity among the shepherds of Israel. They have taken care of themselves rather than the flock of God. They have failed in strengthening the weak, healing the sick, and binding up the wounded. They have let the strays go, and they have not searched for the lost. They have abused and misused their power. The flock became the prey of all manner of wild animals. Thus, God lays claim to the shepherding vocation. In so doing, a job description is given of the pastoral vocation: "I myself will be the shepherd of my sheep, and I will make them lie down, says the Lord God. I will seek the lost, and I will bring back the strayed, and I will bind up the injured, and I will strengthen the weak, but the fat and the strong I will destroy [or watch over, depending on the version of the text]. I will feed them with justice" (vv. 15–16). Again, here is a reminder that it is God who is at work as the shepherd of God's people. But a more precise job description for the pastoral vocation in which one participates with God cannot be found in all of scripture.

An informative epistle text is from Paul's great letter to the Ephesians (4:1–7, 11–16). This is a reminder for the pastor to live a life worthy of the calling, to maintain the unity of the Spirit in the bond of peace. The ordained ministry is to equip the saints for the work of ministry and to build up the body of Christ. This is a charge for the pastor never to forget and always to value the sacredness of Christian community, the church, the body of Christ in the world. Ministry is the work of reconciliation, the work of teaching and preaching, the guiding of the people of God into the deepening of the faith and the maturity of love. This calls for the pastor to be a teacher, preacher, and scholar to the end. Here is the clarity for the pastoral vocation. Do not let busyness replace reflectiveness or shallowness replace depth in the exercise of the vocation.

Two texts from the gospels shed particular light on the issue of pastoral clarity in a desert context. The first text describes an event from the beginning of the ministry of Jesus, and the second text discloses a conversation near the end of his ministry, spoken in the shadow of the cross.

Luke 4:1–15 is the story of Jesus' temptation in the wilderness of Judea and stands as a reminder that the life of ministry is full of temptation. The narrative reveals three temptations: (1) the temptation to the abuse of power for one's own satisfaction and glorification; (2) the temptation to a false ministry; and (3) the temptation to trust in oneself rather than God. This encounter of Jesus in the desert at the beginning of his ministry is a reminder that the only counter to these temptations is a life centered in the word of God and prayer. The house of prayer and the citadel of the word of God combine to make the dwelling place for the pastoral vocation.

The second text from the gospel is Mark 10:35–45. This narrative is a reminder that the lust for prestige and prominence is never far from the pastor's heart. In this text Jesus reminds the disciples that there is a cup to be drunk and a baptism with which to be baptized if one is to follow his way in the world. That way is then defined as servanthood.

> "You know that among the Gentiles those whom they recognize as their rulers lord it over them, and their great ones are tyrants over them. But it is not so among you; but whoever wishes to become great among you must be your servant, and whoever wishes to be first among you must be slave of all. For the Son of Man came not to be served but to serve, and to give his life a ransom for many." (vv. 42b–45).

All these biblical images, narratives, and metaphors combine to illustrate the issues of pastoral clarity that we have been addressing to this point. The vocation of ministry is a holiness and a gift; it is being a voice for justice for those who have no voice; it is a calling to compassion and service; it is directed to the healing of the wounded, the finding of the lost, the binding up of the broken, and the nurturing of all in justice; it is the work of scholarship and proclamation and teaching; it is the constant struggle against the abuse of power, the resistance to the temptation of false ministry, and the surrender of one's life to trust in God; it is a life lived in prayer and the strong word of God; it is a life marked by servanthood.

Functioning from the Foundations

So far in this chapter we have been exploring the theological foundations of the pastoral vocation in somewhat abstract ways. We now turn our attention to five functional ways one can begin to live out this vocation with clarity, passion, and integrity.

1. The Pastor as Person

One enters this sacred vocation first and foremost as the person one is—in one's own personhood. This is the first mark of authenticity in pastoral vocational clarity. Be who you are and who you are called to be as Christ's person. Be true to yourself in light of your faith. You are not called to be some other. What Parker Palmer says of vocation in general is also true of the pastoral vocation: "Is the life I am living the same life that wants to live in me?"[7] You are not called to develop a "pastoral persona" that is deemed to be acceptable to others' pious expectations but false to yourself. Who you are as pastor should correspond to who you are as person.

Too often the personhood of the pastor is lost by the pastor's allowing herself or himself to "become" the functionary of the church's goals, plans, programs, and agendas. Too late one discovers when one reaches to the center of one's being that there is nothing there. There is no center; there are no nonnegotiables of one's own personhood, no self. When this happens, we have exchanged the mystery of ministry to persons by persons in the presence of the three-person God for the predictable manipulation of members of the organization. You are first and foremost called "to be" and "to become" before you "do" anything.

This is not suggesting radical individualism, but authentic personhood. Carlyle Marney makes this distinction: "The individual is the self with its things. The person is the self with the selves who created and called the person out."[8] Your personhood is your self-in-relationship. To be a person is no longer simply to be an individual. This is, of course, rooted in the doctrine of the Trinity to which I referred earlier—God is God in and through social relationships.

Treating oneself with sacred care is not selfishness. It is the first mandate for ethical behavior in the pastoral vocation. Ethics emerge from character, and character is one's personhood. C. S.

Lewis poignantly touched this theme in some words he wrote into the flyleaf of his copy of Baron von Hugel's *Eternal Life*:

> It is not an abstraction called Humanity that is to be saved. It is you...your soul, and in some sense yet to be understood, even your body, that was made for the high and holy place. All that you are...every fold and crease of your individuality was devised from all eternity to fit God as a glove fits a hand. All that intimate particularity you can hardly grasp yourself, much less communicate to your fellow creatures, is no mystery to him. He made those ins and outs that he might fill them. Then he gave your soul so curious a life because it is the key designed to unlock that door, of all the myriad doors in him.[9]

Attention to one's own life, one's own personhood, one's own voice, one's own character, not only gives authenticity and integrity to one's pastoral vocation and makes genuine relationships possible, but it is the key to the spiritual life. One's own life is the key that unlocks the door to "all the myriad doors in God." Rabbi Zusya illuminated this reality when he said upon nearing death, "In the world to come I shall not be asked: 'Why was I not Moses?' I shall be asked: 'Why were you not Zusya?'"[10]

Who one is in relationship to God, oneself, and others is likely to be more important for the long-distance run of the pastoral vocation than what one does. This is so because what one does will flow out of who one is. And such is the mystery of the pastoral vocation that the pastor will often be called to "do less" and "be more." In times of distress, anxiety, and extremity, people seek presence rather than performance.

2. The Pastor as Servant

One of the textual images used earlier in this chapter was the classic gospel text on servanthood. To bind oneself to Christ's way of being in the world is to be a servant. This is most definitely not a degrading designation nor a call to be the pious doormat on which others can wipe their feet. It is, to be exact, to be strong in rendering service. Serving takes on the same dynamics in relationship to life as does worship. It does so in this fashion. It is not a question of whether one worships or not; everyone worships at some altar. It is a question of the object of one's worship; all people serve even as all people worship. The question is the object of one's service.

We have stated again and again that the quintessential shorthand way of speaking of the pastoral vocation is the phrase "minister of word and sacrament." "Minister," of course, comes from the Greek word for servant. As pastors we are called to be servants of the word of God and servants of the people of God. In both these capacities we are called to be servants of the God who speaks and the God who calls a people into existence for the sake of God's love for the world—for the sake of community in love, freedom, and justice. The focus of pastoral servanthood is to be lived in two directions: (1) attention to the seven marks of the church that are reflected in the ordination promises, and (2) attention to the people of God as interpreters and mediators of the graces of the gospel in the actual lived experiences of their lives. To be the pastor as servant is thus to give equal attention to "living in the word/prayer/liturgy of the spiritual life" and "living among the people in their needs and fulfillments, longings and disappointments, sorrows and joys." In so doing the pastoral life will be focused in God, and pastoral tasks will be devoted to keeping the people attentive to God.

Eugene Peterson boils down this servant task to three commitments.[11] The pastor, he says, is to pray, preach, and listen. The pastor prays, for all ministry begins with God. The pastor preaches, for here the gospel is announced and existence is interpreted toward meaning in light of the gospel. The pastor listens among the people, for the pastor not only represents God to the people, but represents the people to God.

Listening, in fact, is the primary mode of servanthood in pastoral living—whether in prayer, in attending to the Word, or in being among the people. This is why Carlyle Marney quipped, "The pastor must listen for seven days for the privilege of talking twenty minutes on a Sunday morning."[12]

3. The Pastor as Living Reminder

Rabbi Heschel said, "Much of what the Bible demands can be comprised in one word: Remember."[13] Nils Dahl, speaking of early Christianity, said, "The first obligation of the apostle *vis a vis* the community—beyond founding it—is to make the faithful remember what they have received and already know—or should know."[14] Henri Nouwen describes the minister as "a living reminder."[15] Drawing on this emphasis on memory, clarity in the pastoral vocation can receive guidance by the conscious decision to minister as "a living reminder" in the following ways:

- Be a living reminder of the healing Christ, that ministry might be a healing ministry.
- Be a living reminder of the sustaining Christ, that ministry might be a sustaining ministry.
- Be a living reminder of the guiding Christ, that ministry might guide in the way of faith and the life of the gospel.
- Be a living reminder of the reconciling Christ, that ministry might be reconciling and bridge building.
- Be a living reminder of the teaching Christ, that ministry might be a teaching ministry.
- Be a living reminder of the serving Christ, that ministry might be a ministry of service.
- Be a living reminder of the holy Christ, that ministry might engage holiness and spirituality.
- Be a living reminder of the loving Christ, that ministry might be grounded in love.
- Be a living reminder of the challenging and prophetic Christ, that ministry might participate in justice and in peace.
- Be a living reminder of the Christ of table fellowship, that ministry might welcome the stranger and the outsider.
- Be a living reminder of the crucified and risen Christ, that ministry will neither sidestep suffering nor forget the promised victory of the One who said, "I have said this to you, so that in me you may have peace. In the world you face persecution. But take courage; I have conquered the world!"[16]

4. The Pastor as Searcher for the Tears of Christ

To avoid all forms of triumphalism in the pastoral vocation and in the church, the pastor is called to be a searcher for the tears of Christ in the world. There were first the tears of Jesus at the beginning of his ministry in the desert of temptation. This reminds us that there is always a death at the beginning of ministry—a death to false authority, a death to false methods, a death to false means, and a death to false goals. The tears wept in the desert at the beginning allowed Jesus to enter the world as servant, as healer, as proclaimer of the good news of God's love, as the artist of authentic community in light of God's grace and justice. And this is where God calls the pastor in, to, and for the church in the world.

But there were also tears at the end of the ministry of Jesus when he wept over Jerusalem. And here the tears come not from his struggle with Satan but from his love for his people. The reason Jesus weeps speaks to us powerfully about the pastoral vocation.

As prince of peace, Christ weeps because we do not know the things that make for peace.

As passionate lover, he weeps for all those who labor and are heavy laden under the burden of their own lives.

As the incarnation of reconciliation, he weeps for every broken tie in family, in friendship, in church, in class, in gender, in nation against nation.

As bridge-building priest, he weeps for every gulf that cannot be bridged and every chasm that cannot be crossed in our relationships with one another and with God.

As healer and physician, he weeps for every wound in existence, every mind in torment, every body in pain, every death to be died.

As bread come down from heaven, he weeps for every stomach that is hungry and every emptiness of heart that is desolate.

As personification of wisdom, he weeps for every hardness of heart, ignorance of mind, and superficiality in existence that bars us from the passion for life.

As friend, he weeps for every loneliness that isolates, every alienation that brings brokenness, every heart that has forgotten or has never learned what it is, means, and feels like to be a friend and to be befriended.

As redeemer and liberator, he weeps for every person who is oppressed by others and every individual who is in bondage to forces she or he can scarcely name.

As Lord and Savior of the world, Christ weeps for every knee that is bowed down to the false gods of our illusions, every soul that is lost, every being that is separated from the ground of being.

In short, Christ weeps for humanity's sorrow, blindness, prejudice, pain, and forgetfulness of the things that make for *shalom*. Christ weeps because he is in love with the world of God's creation. And where Christ's tears drop is where the pastor leads the church in ministry, for there is where the healing, redeeming, and reconciling love of God goes searching. As minister of word and sacrament, called to join in the work of God in the world, the pastor is a searcher for the tears of Christ.

5. *The Pastor as Grassroots Theologian in the Community*

Finally, the pastor is called to be among the people as a theologian. The urgency of this calling in the current desert experience cannot be overemphasized. To a large extent the interest in, discipline for, and attention to the theological task at the grassroots level in the congregations has been abandoned by their pastors.

The theological pastor's function within the church and world is to live the "what" and the "so what" questions of faith and life in light of the gospel. What are the realities of human life lived in a given time and place in history? What are the questions, philosophical assumptions, and alternate stories vying to shape human life? What are the principalities and powers impinging on human freedom? What are the idols demanding allegiance that define this desert experience? What are the day-to-day particularities within which church members and nonmembers alike are living? What are the challenges and barriers to love, freedom, and justice within the community? And what is the call of faith in light of the gospel in this particular context? Once the "what" questions are wrestled with theologically, the theological pastor will turn her or his attention to the "so what" questions. So what difference does all of this make in who we are, how we believe, what we do, and how we live? So what are the consequences of all of this to our humanity? So what does the story of Jesus mean in all of this?

The theological pastor is to make the journey with the people of God along that strange path where, in classical terms, their "faith is in search of understanding." But in a time when our parishioners' "understandings" may far outstrip their faith—understandings drawn from the physical, psychological, and social sciences—the theological task may be to explore understandings in search of faith. This kind of theological work must be at the center of the church's new mission in the world.

The challenge of being a grassroots theologian is that pastoral theological work cannot be done from a safe distance or tenured protection. Nor is it done from a position of spiritual superiority. The pastor is simply the one, by virtue of calling and training, designated to perform this task within the community, helping the community itself to think theologically. If this task is abandoned, it is at the price of the pastoral calling and at the peril of the church.

It is "late in the day" for serious theological engagement at the local church level, and there is a good deal of anti-intellectual, antitheological sentiment within some congregations and sectors of the church. This makes the recognition of the importance of this task on the part of contemporary pastors all the more urgent. A word of warning, however, is in order for those pastors who desire to be faithful in this aspect of the pastoral vocation. First, in doing theology at the grassroots level, there is no room for arrogance or pomposity. In this context more than anywhere else, theology is done in the service of the church. The pastor does not "impose" a theology. Inviting the congregation into participation in the task, and beginning with the congregation's own "what" questions, is both a beneficial manner of theological existence within the church and a resource of quite profound and insightful subject matter. The other word of warning is simply that when one does theology in direct relationship with a living community of faith, there are some risks involved! But if faith is risk rather than certitude, this is the risk inherent in the calling of the theological pastor. As Samuel Miller, former dean of Harvard Divinity School, put it in a sermon:

> A person of faith is bound to be a person on the way, a visitor, the eternal "sojourner on earth," who has here below "no abiding city." One knows not; one believes. One has not; one hopes for; one sees not; one obeys. And this road is not defined like the unvarying orbit of a star, but is permanently venture; it is created under the feet of those who take it.[17]

Carlyle Marney, one who took the theological dimensions of the pastoral vocation seriously, recognized the risks, and in commenting on Miller's sermon warned all pastors, with prescient accuracy, "Faith here becomes 'active confidence' living 'essential anxiety.'"[18] The active confidence of faith dares to believe that the theological "path" through these desert times will be created under the feet of the pastors and congregations who step out in this direction in courage.

CHAPTER 6

A Regula Pastorum *for Contemporary Pastors*

A *Regula Pastorum* is simply a "rule for pastors," a rule of life and vocation. In the Protestant traditions we are not accustomed to speaking in terms of a "rule." We do not, for example, take on something comparable to the Benedictine Rule or the Rule of the Franciscans. We do not take the traditional vows of chastity, obedience, and poverty. However, we do take certain vows and make certain promises within the context of our ordination to Christian ministry.

Unfortunately, we often do not pay very careful attention to these vows in the actual practice of ministry in the years that follow our day of ordination. One of the purposes of this conversation with ordinands and pastors is to raise this precise issue. A *Regula Pastorum* is one way we can provide ourselves with guidance in paying attention to the focus of our pastoral work, thus bringing more clarity to the daily and weekly tasks we perform. Such a rule is not meant to be a heavy burden or to make us feel guilty. It is meant to be a means of grace through which the yoke of Christ can be "lighter."[1] Pastors simply carry more than needs to be carried. There is much we can lay aside in order that we might be more authentic in the vocation.

What follows is offered not as a blueprint rule for all pastors but as the guide I have developed for myself through the years of my ministry. It is the result of attempting to learn from my failures and sins (theological and otherwise!). I present it here for the purpose of encouraging colleagues to revisit their own theological foundations for ministry, their own images of ministry, and their own current practice of ministry with an eye to preparing their own *Regula Pastorum.*

The Rule

I. I bind myself to the cultivation of the spiritual life.

This will involve:

A. Daily prayer, in which I make an unbreakable appointment with God.

B. Daily meditation on a brief passage of scripture in relationship to my own life.

C. Reading in and reflecting on the classics of Christian spirituality.

D. The regular "*examin* of conscience," accompanied by repentance and acts of contrition.

E. An annual retreat focusing on my own care, my own spiritual life and needs.

II. I bind myself to focus my ministry in being a theological pastor.

This will involve:

A. Concentrating on the tasks of prayer, preaching, listening, and engagement in the disciplines that support these acts of ministry.

B. Weighing all pastoral responsibilities accepted in light of whether they express my vocation as a servant of word and sacrament and a servant of the people through word and sacrament.

C. Dividing my time equally, as much as is possible, between private study, reading, and prayer on the one hand and pastoral care among the people on the other hand.

D. Focusing my "speaking" on the liberating, freeing, forgiving, loving good news of the gospel of Jesus Christ. I will attempt to make my "speaking" both biblical and relevant, believing that biblical speaking is relevant and relevant speaking is biblical.

E. Engaging in systematic theological reflection on my practice of ministry and on the ministry of the church in the world. I will strive for wholeness and balance over against the reductionism of one-issue–oriented theology and practice.

F. Reading and studying for my own nurture and growth at other times than when I am "preparing to present" something in public.

G. Attempting, as much as is possible, to make sure that teaching precedes change in the life of my congregation.

III. **Among the people, I bind myself to the following.**

A. To the best of my ability I will do no harm. I will recognize the limitations of my abilities and expertise.

B. I will attempt to live with patient endurance in my ministry (especially in the days of frustration and disappointment and hurt and suffering and anger with the meanness of people, the foibles and foolishness of my own life and the life of the church, and the terrible brokenness of the world).

C. I will attempt to control my anger, bitterness, and despair, including finding the appropriate places and people with whom to vent and appropriate resources for professional help when needed.

D. With God's help I will love my people and be available to provide pastoral care. I will recognize that it is out of authentic pastoral care and genuine love of the people that the prophetic voice and challenge can be spoken.

E. I will allow my people to love me and be open to receiving the gifts and help their lives offer me.

F. I will give diligence to the control of my tongue, giving respect at all times to the power and sacredness of language. I will attempt to keep my language from either demeaning people or being demeaned itself by being emptied of authentic meaning. I will attempt to keep both my everyday language and my theological language from being cheapened or abused by either the inflation of claims or the desecration of meaninglessness. I will attempt to "let my yes be yes and my no be no."

G. I will respect the personhood of all people and will resist the abuse of my pastoral position for personal, financial, sexual, or psychological gratification.

IV. **Among my colleagues in ministry, I bind myself to the following principles.**

A. I will value the practice of collegiality and will seek to live in mutual encouragement.

B. I will avoid competition and the temptation to boasting or complaining.
C. I will seek to avail myself of a confessor with whom to confess my sins and to be available to act as confessor for others.

V. With respect to my own personhood, I commit myself to the following goals.

A. I will live with personal integrity.
B. I will be true to myself and my convictions, resisting the threats to my own personhood.
C. I will understand that faith is risk. I make this commitment understanding that our risks sometimes lead us into suffering, complexity, and even sin, but sometimes also into tremendous breakthroughs, wonderful growth, great joy, and unfathomable discoveries.
D. I will cultivate a quiet confidence in myself through faith in God's merciful gift of uniqueness.
E. I will be open to change and correction as times, circumstances, the leading of the Holy Spirit, and new insights, discoveries, and understanding indicate.
F. I will love myself and care for myself and my needs, including play, relaxation, and the cultivation of supportive and nourishing friendships.
G. I will love my family, care for them, and be available to them.
H. I will understand success only in terms of faithfulness.
I. I will keep alive and celebrate the incredible wonder and surprise of life, of the gospel, and of God's unconditional love for me and others.

VI. I bind myself to Godwardness.

In relationship to my pastoral vocation this means:
A. Recognizing my utter dependence on God for life, ministry, and redemption.
B. Paying attention to my own faith journey, including its doubts, in order to "speak" my ministry with pastoral vocational integrity rather than with professional career convenience.
C. Confessing that from beginning to end it is God's ministry. God is already at work in creative,

redemptive, liberative, and transformative ways. I join in this ministry as an earthen vessel and receive this ministry as a gift.

D. Resolving to leave this ministry in the hands of God. It does not all depend on me. To God belong the outcome, the results, the harvest, and the eschaton. To God alone belong the issues of life and death. To God alone belongs the glory.

* * *

The discerning reader will recognize that the above rule is not a statement of fact about the author's ministry! It is a hope, a desire, a guide. It is a goal that contributes to my own vocational clarity and provides a stationary point for the pivot of my own compass, a tool to be used in my own *examin* of conscience.

Two Questions

In writing a *Regula Pastorum,* two questions should be raised for prolonged meditation in listening to one's own life. The questions were raised by Albert Curry Winn in an ordination sermon entitled "The Plainest and Simplest Thing in the World."

First, do you know that God has loved you? Have you sensed the sweep and wonder of what happened in Jesus? Second, are you trying to find God so you can love God back? Because if you are, you will find your people. You may go a long road, sweeping the heavens and plumbing the depths, looking for God. God is there in transcendence, but you will not see God. God will set God's self before you in the people. And if you know you have been loved, you will learn to love. [2]

Saint Augustine pointed to this reality when he considered the Christic presence in his vision of the two aspects of Christ.

Christ is at once above and below; above in Christness, below in people; above with God, below in us. Fear Christ above, recognize Christ below. Have Christ above bestowing bounty, recognize Christ here in need. Here Christ is poor, there Christ is rich. So then, Christ is rich and poor. Christ hath ascended into heaven, and sitteth at the right hand of God; yet is Christ still poor here, is ahungered, and athirst. [3]

A Personal Message to Ordinands

As God's person, called and ordained by the church to the pastoral vocation as a minister of word and sacrament, stake your claim with humble boldness in desert hearts. You are a desert pilgrim. But you are a desert pilgrim as an ambassador of Christ. Christ is your only authority—Christ's method your only means, Christ's vision of God's reign your only goal, Christ's gospel your only word. Be among the people in your pastoral care as *paraclete, philos, diaconia, hierus, didaskalos, poimen,* and *kerux*—as counselor, friend, servant, priest, teacher, pastor, and preacher.

May your eyes be opened to see God's image deep in every person. May your ears be attentive to the cry of every hurting heart. May your tongue resound with the voice of the voiceless. May your hands be gentle to break the bread and lift the cup and take the towel and the basin among your sisters and brothers in service. And may your lips be blessed to speak no word but gospel truth. With the cross above you, your baptism behind you, the table of the Lord before you, the scriptures beside you, the Holy Spirit within you, and the people of God around you, may you

> with your unconstraining voice
> still persuade us to rejoice;
> with the farming of a verse
> make a vineyard of the curse;
> in the prison of our days,
> teach us how to praise.[4]

PART TWO

Healing
Fountains
in the
Pastoral
Vocation

CHAPTER 7

The Pastor under Many and Varied Conditions

I received my first Bible when I was born. It was from Chaplain Edwin Hampton, Lieutenant, 394th Infantry Division, United States Army. He inscribed it: "To Victor…This little book is a safe guide." Two years after I received my first Bible, my parents received their last letter from Chaplain Hampton. It was a V-Mail, dated November 20, 1944, somewhere in France. It said, in part:

> It may be interesting to you to know that I have held worship services each Sunday since I left the States under many and varied conditions. I have held them on deck in the Atlantic. I have held them in a hayloft in a barn. I have held them out in open fields in the snow. But not one time have we missed having worship. It makes me appreciate the fact that God's people can exist anywhere God's people are. May the Lord bless and keep all of you and may the rest of this year and the new year bring safety and peace to us all, is my prayer.

One month later Chaplain Edwin Hampton was killed in the Battle of the Bulge. I still keep the Bible and the V-Mail together on the mantle of the fireplace in my study.

Combined, they have become a kind of parable for me of the pastoral vocation. A first book and a last letter. A first blessing and a final prayer. Side by side. A book that encompasses all of life in its many and varied conditions—but ultimately a book of hope and faith, grace and love, and the steadfastness of God. A letter written out of the depths of war and violence, human suffering and fear, death and dreadful loss—but ultimately a letter that encompasses life in its many and varied conditions.

What held the letter of life and the book of life together was a chaplain who prayed, pastored, and worshiped under many and varied conditions. A pastor who held the book of grace in one hand and the bitterness of war in the other. A pastor holding worship in a geography of wasting, speaking hope in a landscape of horror, offering faith in the fields of fear, giving compassion in a context of the cursed. A pastor sustaining truth in a terrain of terror, having humility in the country of the unanswerable and the inconceivable, and celebrating sacrament in the sharp-edged shale of suffering. A pastor sharing companionship in the valley of the shadow and being present in the void of absence.

Pastoring is a work that takes place under many and varied conditions. It occurs in many contexts and settings. It takes place in private and in public. The work of the pastoral vocation occurs when no one is watching and when everyone is watching.

Chaplain Hampton knew that in these many and varied conditions of human life, the center of the pastoral work is worship. He knew the task, whatever the condition and wherever the surroundings, is to hold human biography and holy book together. The pastor is a contact point, a bridge (*pontifex*, "priest"), at the intersection of the human and divine stories.

Reinhold Niebuhr was a pastor for thirteen years in Detroit before taking a teaching post at Union Theological Seminary in New York. His years of work as a pastor are reflected in the classic volume *Leaves from the Notebook of a Tamed Cynic.* In the preface of that collection of pastoral reflections he writes: "I pay my tribute to the calling [of parish pastor], firm in the conviction that it offers greater opportunities for both moral adventure and social usefulness than any other calling, if it is entered with open eyes and a consciousness of the hazards to virtue which lurk in it."[1] Whatever Niebuhr may have had in mind, surely one of the great and persistent hazards to virtue in the pastoral ministry is forgetting the nature of the vocation.

One of the reasons clarity in the pastoral vocation is so crucial is exactly because it takes place under many and varied conditions, in many and varied circumstances, with many and varied people, involving many and varied issues, resulting in many and varied outcomes. It is the discipline of vocational clarity that pushes toward a singleness of heart under such diverse realities.

Pastoral clarity helps the pastor hold it all together—not only when the pastor is working under the many and varied conditions of the people, but out of the many and varied conditions of the pastor's own heart and life. The pastor is not immune to being up and down, joyful and sorrowful, healthy and ill, positive and negative, apathetic and passionate, at peace and in anger. The pastor is not immune to the struggles of faith and doubt, courage and cowardice. But the pastoral ministry is not exercised out of the whims of the pastor's present moods but out of the sure word of God and the faithful sacramental presence of Christ.

"In the deserts of the heart/Let the healing fountain start." The healing fountains of pastoral work are not in the power of the pastoral personality but in the living water of God's divine grace. But pastoral vocational clarity, even in the midst of the many and varied conditions of desert hearts and desert travel, provides the conduit through which that water can flow. That is, the healing fountains can flow through the life of the pastor if the pastor keeps the conduit of vocational focus unclogged from the debris of confusion. This process of vocational clarification is chiefly a matter of what the pastor attends to in the daily and weekly exercise of the ministry.

In order to hold together the gospel story and the human stories in a framework of interpreting existence toward meaning and offering life—in order to address the fundamental theological question, "What is the word that gives life?"—the pastor's habits need to be centered in attending to self, attending to God, and attending to others. Acting wisely in the detailed tasks of parish life and the complexities of human hope and need emerges from the pastor's attentive habits rather than frantic action. Being helpful in forming and nurturing a community of grace and life is possible only when the focused attention of the pastor is on grace and life.

The pastor needs to attend to his or her own life and needs. There needs to be a constant process of re-creating the body, the mind, and the spirit. Self-care among pastors is, I believe, an ethical mandate, but it is often ignored. In Thornton Wilder's marvelous play *Our Town*, Emily, who has died, is allowed to visit her life on her seventeenth birthday. She is astounded at everyone's inattention to their lives. She asks her escort, "Does anyone see life when they are living it?" He answers, "Not many; saints and a few poets." And, we would hope to add, a few pastors. Life happens, but do we see it? Life happens, but do we attend to it? Paying attention to one's own life is the basis of reflective theological and pastoral practice.

The pastor also needs to attend to God. We are talking about the spiritual life, and it is out of the spiritual life and the pastor's attention to God that faithful pastors live and speak. One of the gifts offered in creation for attending to the Creator—and the relationship between the Creator and the created—is Sabbath. Sabbath is for paying attention. Sabbath is to make visible that we are not primarily producers and consumers, but worshipers. Sabbath is to provide a holiday or holy day from anxiety. Sabbath is both a day and a spiritual practice.[2] I recently heard the story of two parents whose eight- and ten-year-old boys simply could not stay out of trouble. They took them to see their pastor, and she agreed to talk with them. She asked to see the ten-year-old first. When he came into her study, she asked him in the course of their conversation, "Where is God?" He immediately bolted from her study, ran home, and hid in the closet. His eight-year-old brother asked him what the matter was. He replied, "We are really in trouble this time. God is missing, and they think we did it!" Sadly, in the secularized and institutionalized running of the church, God is often missing, and pastors may have had something to do with it. The pastoral vocation involves attending to God. The practice of Sabbath is a means of paying attention. It is made for us, according to Jesus,[3] but pastors rarely avail themselves of the gift of Sabbath.

Finally, the pastor needs to attend to others. Specifically, attending to others means attending to the particularity in the lives of those in your pastoral care under their many and varied conditions. It involves not just generalizations about humanity and its conditions, but precise attentiveness to persons and their concerns and contexts. It is to follow the discipline of this aphorism from Western spirituality: *agi quod agis*—do what you are doing; pay attention to the present, to the ordinary, to the particular.

In a course with Seward Hiltner, one of the giants in pastoral theology who was ever insistent that the task of pastoral care and counseling be rooted in the practice of theology, I learned the importance of particularity in attending to others. An exchange between Hiltner and Paul Tillich at the University of Chicago illustrates the point. They were making a presentation together, and the exchange went something like this.

Tillich: "Let us say that there was a certain man…"

Hiltner (interrupting): "What was his name?"

Tillich: "Oh…er…let us say John. So there was this man named John and…"

Hiltner (interrupting): "Was he married?"

Tillich: "Let us say that he was. So, there was this married man John, who…"

Hiltner (interrupting again): "What was his wife's name? Did they both work?"

Tillich (with exasperation): "Professor Hiltner, won't you please let me finish? What is the meaning of all your questions?"

Hiltner: "To speak of just *any* man is to speak of no man at all!"[4]

Attention to self. Attention to God. Attention to others. Paying attention focuses the living water from healing fountains on thirsty lips. The aim and goal of the pastoral vocation is "quenching the thirst" of specific persons and communities, not delivering abstractions. "Ho, everyone who thirsts, come to the waters; and you that have no money, come, buy and eat!…Why do you spend your money for that which is not bread, and your labor for that which does not satisfy? Listen carefully to me, and eat what is good, and delight yourselves in rich food. Incline your ear, and come to me; listen, so that you may live."[5] This invitation to the thirsty in Isaiah is especially applicable to pastors in today's ministry. In a time when we chase after new techniques and programs to make our pastorates successful and our churches grow, the question "Why spend money on what is not bread, and your labor on what does not satisfy?" probes to the very heart of our pastoral confusion. Paying attention will go a long way in helping with our clarity in the vocation.

The remaining chapters will explore these healing fountains of pastoral ministry in order that our souls might live. The purpose will not be to explore the skills necessary to the fulfillment of these pastoral tasks (there are many excellent books, articles, and courses on the skills), but to explore the habits and frameworks of the pastoral life that will enable the pastor to weave the tasks of ministry under many and varied conditions into an overall tapestry of pastoral vocational clarity.

CHAPTER 8

The Pastor and Worship

Worship is the center and circumference of parish life. The gathering of the people of God in word and sacrament is the constituting act of the Christian congregation. Jesus spoke of being present "where two or three are gathered in [his] name."[1] The "in-commonness" of the earliest Pentecostal community was marked by attending "to the apostles' teaching and fellowship, to the breaking of bread and the prayers."[2] The Hebrew letter to pilgrims encouraged frequent gathering together for exhortation to love and good works.[3] Ignatius followed this emphasis in the early second century: "Give diligence therefore to come together more frequently for thanksgiving *(eucharistia)* and glory to God, for when you are frequently together in one place, the powers of Satan are destroyed and his destructiveness is nullified by the concord of your faith."[4] Frank Senn has pointed to the centrality of liturgy to the life of the church in every century, including its theological life and its life of witness and proclamation in the world.[5]

Today's Christian congregations cannot abandon what has been central in every century to the Christian community's way of being in the world. That way of being is as a worshiping community celebrating the love of God and the presence of Jesus. This sacramental reality is made visible in the gathered community of faith at the Lord's table and in the Lord's Word. It extends into the church in diaspora in every aspect of life in the Lord's world. Worship is *all* the Christian congregation does—the church only worships; and everything the church does in terms of social action, care, evangelism, prophetic ministry, and education is worship. There are seven or eight Greek words in the New Testament used to convey the idea of worship. They range in meaning from reverence, awe, and devotion to service, lifestyle, giving, and social action. We have tried to squeeze those meanings into the one word and in so doing have lost both the breadth and depth of the meaning of worship. Thus, the church's ministries in the world are in danger of being reduced to humanitarian good works, and its services in the sanctuary tend toward pious "pep rallies" for Christian witness. In both cases the church loses its nature as a sacramental sign of the presence of Christ in the world.

Lack of clarity in the pastoral vocation has contributed to this disaster. As we have seen, religious busyness robs the pastor of the theological vocation. The theological vocation is one of prayer and worship, which shape theological reflection. This has been appreciated from the earliest centuries of the church. The patristic phrase *lex orandi, lex credendi*[6] expresses the fact that theology and worship interact with each other. Prayer and belief are reciprocal. "What Christians believe affects the manner in which they pray and worship; the manner in which Christians pray and worship affects what they believe."[7] How can a pastor's vocational clarity in regard to worship begin to lead the people of God to those healing fountains where the *leitourgia* (the work of the people of God) can be nourished by the refreshing waters of the wellsprings of faith, not dictated by the whims of personal taste and needs-based "liturgical fantasy"?

From Personal Tastes to Adoration of God

The pastor's own attentiveness to God and willingness to help the congregation in its great variety of ages, tastes, educational backgrounds, and cultural experiences recovers the object of worship—the adoration of God. Because of the widespread sellout to culture by our churches, it will take great focus to move contemporary church members in their corporate worship, whatever the style, from preoccupation with themselves and the titillation of their own individual "tastes" to the praise of God. Pastors often replace the liturgy of prayer, praise, confession, repentance, absolution, word, and sacrament with what they hope makes people feel good, excites them, entertains them, and keeps them coming back. The focus is placed on the different "audiences" for the "worship experience"—revealing an immediate betrayal of the principle of congregants communing with God and parishioners participating in divine worship for the idea of "spectators at a jolly good show"!

I realize this is not the intention, but I believe it is the outcome of worship designed to meet the needs of all the people, whether, in those terribly misleading terms, they are of a "traditional" or a "contemporary" nature. Even the well-intended approach of "blending worship" keeps the focus on the people and their tastes rather than on God and God's transforming glory.

The Renewal of Ritual

Because the pastoral vocation is to keep the people attentive to God, then not only is moving the focus of worship back to God and away from personal predilections in taste required, but so is a new attention to the role and renewal of ritual. The goal of ritual is to help to powerfully anchor all of life in God in the human journey from birth to death. It is true that rituals can be emptied of their meaning and become rote expressions in substitute of living faith. Jaroslav Pelikan's familiar quip that "Traditions are the living faith of the dead and traditionalism is the dead faith of the living" remains true. But it is the renewal of ritual, not its abandonment, that is necessary pastoral work. Without common rituals and a participation in common symbols, no community is possible. This is especially true of a community whose understanding of life is that it flows from God, in God, to God, therefore drawing together a shared past, a collective present, and a hoped-for future. The redemptive journey in Christian faith is not that of the lone pilgrim but of the caravan of mutual sojourners. The privatization of worship is contributing greatly to the individualization of spirituality, and if not the destruction of community, at least its polarization.

Ritual has a conserving function and a renewing function,[8] both of which are extremely important for pastors to address in this desert situation and time of ecclesial lack of identity. According to Roland Delattre, its conserving function is to provide anchorage and articulation; its renewing function is to provide negotiation and passage.[9]

In the church, "anchorage" would certainly involve the faith community's connection with the past. The church did not start with us. We don't simply make it up as we go along, and not everything worth doing or knowing was discovered in the last decade. This is the great illusion of progress. I recently received a telephone call in my study in which a woman demanded, "Do you use contemporary music?" Some irresistible urge made me reply, "Not if you mean something that was written in the last fifteen minutes." It is the pastor's vocational responsibility to enhance this conserving element in the church, this anchorage, by giving attention to the texts, creeds, confessions, liturgies, hymns, interpretations, and traditions of the community of faith in the past and to give them ritual expression in the present. But more than a connection with the past, anchorage must be in the present as well. This is what renewed ritual can do in a living community. It means that we are not subject to every prevailing fad. The worshiping pilgrim community that must move through this desert experience in the caravan of *koinonia* may well be on the move—in fact, must be on the move—but it is not groundless, uncentered, and unconnected. Common ritual and shared symbols provide this anchorage.

The second conserving function of ritual is articulation. In other words, it helps the church to "speak" its faith. This speaking is done through art, music, oration, and drama. Articulation is one of the functions of liturgy—the ritualization of the faith through such common articulations as confession (to acknowledge together), baptism, eucharist, shared prayers, litanies, and so forth. The story of faith is to be conserved if it is to be remembered and lived. Ritual provides a means of common preservation, central plot, and shared articulation.

But ritual is also important to the church's movement and change. The church is not an institution but a dynamic community. It has always had to negotiate its way through new cultures, new circumstances, new learnings, and new challenges. And what is true of the church is also true of its members. Life is not static. Life itself, at the individual as well as the community level, must be negotiated. The first renewing function of ritual is the process of negotiation. Through such ritual acts as confession and absolution (corporate and individual) and storytelling within the community, new ways and new possibilities can be opened to the future that were once closed. The use of ritual in a renewing way can help the whole community as well as the individual relationships within the community to move ahead without fracturing, destroying, or fragmenting.

The other renewing function of ritual is passage. Both communities and individuals go through many passages—birth, childhood, adolescence, young adulthood, middle age, old age, death. They also process through marriages, divorces, separations, illnesses, leaving home, establishing a home, and so forth. And there are, of course, weddings, funerals, baptisms, confirmations, birthdays, anniversaries, coming of age, and many other daily crises and joys that accompany the human journey. Ritualizing these events can give meaning to both continuity and change in life, helping with the inevitable goodbyes, transitions, and new beginnings in life.

The pastor with clear vocational identity knows that worship is the central act of the Christian community in which the community's life is centered in God. The pastor's recovery and renewal of ritual within the corporate life of the community and within the individual lives of the members of the community provides stability without rigidity and serves change without mindless anarchy. The pastor's role as reminder and interpreter of the common symbols of the faith serves the congregation well in its quest for ecclesial identity and authentic participatory community. It contributes to a recapturing of the sanctification of life, relationships, time, and space in a culture and a church that has capitulated to the secularization of our age. Life can once again be lived with a sense of holiness, reflecting both joy and sobriety, celebration and suffering—the mysterious mix at the heart of a distinctively Christian sensitivity to life. When the pastor focuses on not simply the means and methods of this or that style of worship but on the meaning and object of worship, the Christian congregation can once again drink from the healing fountains that refresh and renew its life together in the rhythms of grace.

We have reached a stage in our conversation where it is becoming evident that pastoral vocational clarity serves to inform the pastor not only of what he or she is to be "doing" on Sundays and between Sundays but also where the actual engaged pastoral tasks feed the vocational clarity of the pastor. This connection of the "being" and "doing" of the pastor and their mutual reinforce-ment of each other gives the pastor's life and ministry ontological integrity. The pastor's being and doing have coherence. We now turn our attention to some of the actual "doings" of the pastor, as liturgist and leader of a community of grace whose constituting act is divine worship. These doings contribute to continued clarity in the vocation as well as to ecclesial identity in the congregation.

These doings are, of course, drawn from the historic marks of the church that clarify the pastoral vocational job description: baptism, preaching, eucharist, prayer, confession and absolution, and suffering. The focus of the exercise of these tasks will be explored in light of the renewal of ritual within the life of the congregation. Since ritual facilitates connection with the past and change to the future, these pastoral tasks will be considered in terms of rites of passage. Anthropologist Arnold van Gennep points out, "For groups, as well as for individuals, life itself means to separate and to be reunited, to change form and condition, to die and to be reborn. It is to act and to cease, to wait and rest, then to begin acting again, but in a different way...there are always new thresholds to cross."[10] According to van Gennep, rites of passage are very much like taking a journey: There is leave taking, passage, and arrival. Such rites of passage would involve preliminary rites (separation), liminal rites (transition), and postliminal rites (incorporation).[11] In light of this scheme, pastoral functions are carried out faithfully when the pastor ministers out of the very core of the gospel narrative: death and resurrection. The pastor provides interpretive companionship in the deaths that must be died, the transitions to resurrection, and the integration and incorporation into new life. The vocational tasks are thereby anchored in the actual paradigm of the gospel rather than in the paradigms of business, institutional management, social work, psychotherapy, group dynamics, or any of the many other paradigms contributing to pastoral vocational confusion. The "tests" by which these "doings" are to be measured are drawn from the Habakkuk questions explored in chapter 5: (1) Does the task bring revelation (interpret existence toward meaning in light of the gospel); (2) does the task give breath (engender life, make life possible)?

Liturgical Functions, Pastoral Functions, and Marks of the Church

Baptism

There have been two practices within the Christian tradition in regard to baptism. One has been the dedication of infants who are then baptized at what has been called the "age of accountability." This is the practice of "adult" baptism, focusing on the personal faith commitment of the one being baptized. If one comes to Christian faith as an adult, all Christian traditions practice adult baptism. It is the rite or ritual of initiation into Christ, into Christ's death and resurrection and into new life in the Christian community. The other tradition has been infant baptism. Here, the celebration of baptism is the act of the church expressing its faith and practice. The child is incorporated into Christ's saving acts and into the life and nurture of the Christian community. The child is raised in the life of the church and led to the act of confirmation. My concern here is not with the form or practice of baptism but with the pastoral function of leading individuals and the community in and through the sacrament of baptism.

Baptism is a crucial rite of passage for entering into the Christian life. It is important liturgically for both the one being baptized and the community. It relates, reviews, and enacts the covenant of love and of forgiveness of sins, portraying our participation in the death and resurrection of Jesus and our rising with him in new life in the company and care of his people.

Pastoral leadership in this act takes time and attention, marking the event of baptism as more than another social event such as joining the scouts or going to a first dance. For the one being baptized and for that family, as well as for the entire congregation, Christian identity is being formed, and responsible caring community is being shaped. The preparation of both the one being baptized and the community in which the baptism is taking place will partake of the preliminal rites, the liminal rite itself in the context of worship, and the postliminal rites. Exploration of what is being left behind, what is dying and what is being said goodbye to and to what end, will form the preliminal rites of this threshold. The baptism itself will be celebrated as the sacred ritual event it is in the context of Christian worship. It will allow all members of the community to revisit their own baptism and affirm their solidarity in faith with the one being baptized. It will allow those strangers to the faith who are among us to ponder and ask questions about the meaning and purpose of it all as the gospel is enacted before them. The postliminal rites will involve the welcoming, acknowledging, and inclusion of the one baptized into the life of the community, in a new way, with intentional symbols and events.

Baptism celebrated and practiced in this fashion under the guidance of a pastor who knows the nature of the vocation becomes not simply an event but an identity-shaping process for both the individual and the congregation. The pastor's clarity helps shape the clarity of the baptismal candidate and the congregation; not only is the sacrament of baptism celebrated but the whole "journey" of faith becomes a sacramental path and process. There really is a "dying and a rising," a taking leave and an·arrival. It is the ritual enactment of the pattern of living for the disciple and the disciple community.

Such a baptismal community interprets life toward meaning in light of the gospel. There are deaths to be died on the journey to authentic personhood in Christ. But death is not the end of the story. New life is possible and comes as a gift to be received. It is received in relational community rather than in the outer limits of loneliness. One belongs; one has a home. One gives what one has to give and receives what one needs to receive in this community of mutuality. In baptism, the *pneuma,* the life-giving breath of the Holy Spirit, is given as gift. The end of this way is life in Christ, and one's future is bound to the future of the resurrected Christ.

Eucharist

The celebration of the eucharist is both ritual event and way of life, being both sacrament and sacramental in the life of the Christian congregation, which is a sign of Christ in the world. The pastor who is clear on the eucharistic vocation of the ordained minister (minister of word and sacrament) leads the congregation to and from the eucharistic table on the Lord's Day to eucharistic living (thankful praise) in the Lord's week. This pastor knows that the bread broken in holy communion is a participation in the body of Christ and that the eucharistic cup shared is a participation in the blood of Christ.[12] The body of Christ that is broken on the Lord's Day at the communion table becomes the body of Christ broken in the world on the six days following.

Eucharistic living flows from eucharistic celebration. It is a life of gracious response to grace received. And the body that is broken for the sake of the world in the six days is reunited and raised up again at the eucharistic table on the first day.

Christian living and Christian witness in the world are then a matter not of humanitarian good works or social action relevance, or even mission programming or benevolent social outreach, but eucharistic presence in places devoid of love, freedom, and justice. This avoids the sense of the strong stooping to help the weak or the righteous giving to the needy in Christian mission. It is a way of Christian life that is truly incarnational, in which the word of God is once again made flesh in the body of Christ in the world. It is "presence" in the best sense of the word in which the Christian community, in all its own broken humanity, comes alongside of and is attentive to mutual sufferings. Eucharistic presence in congregational life is lived as open invitation to the table—both the communion table of the Lord's Day and the common table of the community's homes. Here life is received as gift and lived as thankful praise.

Vocational clarity on the part of the pastor will help the pastor lead the people of God from eucharistic table to eucharistic living to eucharistic table. This is the rhythm of Christian living and corporate life in Christ. It involves an all-encompassing vision that begins with Christ's table fellowship in his ministry (his indiscriminate, or promiscuous, eating) to his Last Supper with the disciples, to his resurrection meals with the apostles, to his promised presence in bread and wine in communion, to his anticipatory invitation to the Messianic banquet in the *eschaton.* The pastor's task is to keep the church attentive to this sacrament and sacramental way of life.

The eucharist is also a weekly rite of passage. The Lord's table and the Lord's Day go together with the Lord's Word in the weekly rhythms of grace in the Christian community. The first day assembly of the people of God is incomplete without holy communion. More and more Protestant denominations and pastors are beginning to realize this and are turning from the sermon as the Protestant event in worship to a recovery of the sacrament of the table as the constituting act of the Christian congregation. Of course, word *and* sacrament go together and interpret each other. But there is a movement away from the church as lecture hall to the church as sanctuary. This is happening, of course, in places other than those that have adopted the entertainment model of worship and the "bait and switch"[13] philosophy of the "seeker service."

The weekly journey to and from the table of the Lord, this rite of passage, involves taking leave of dilemmas, sins, injuries, and failures of the past week. It is confession. It is to cease acting and doing and working in order to wait and rest. It is Sabbath, and it is re-creation. It is reunification with Christ and with sisters and brothers. And it is then to enter into life again, forgiven and freed, renewed and thankful, fed with the body and blood of Christ.

Once again, the eucharistic action in the eucharistic community is the place where life is interpreted toward meaning in light of the gospel. It is the place of revelation. It is the place for "catching one's breath" in the life-engendering presence of Christ. This is why the apostle Paul connects the abuse of eucharistic practice or the failure of eucharistic practice with ill health and death in the Christian congregation.[14]

Preaching

The pastor with vocational clarity will know that preaching the gospel is a central task for the minister of word and sacrament. "Catch as catch can" preaching, as a result of time spent in busyness throughout the week, is unfaithful to the ordination vows and unfair to the congregation who is to be a hearing and responding fellowship to the word of God. When the time and discipline needed for preparation to preach the gospel are neglected, the eventual result is the "gutting" of Christian community, the breaking down of its foundations, the disappearance of its identity, and the spiritual shallowness of its life.

If the congregation is gathered as response to the invitation of Christ, shaped by the word of Christ, and sent forth into mission with the message of Christ, what happens when pastors fail in the announcing of that invitation, the preaching of that word, and the sending forth with the meaning of that message? The dissolution of clarity in regard to gospel preaching as a central task of gospel ministry among the clergy results in ecclesial confusion, congregational malaise, and community disorientation. Gospel preaching that breaks a hard heart and heals a broken heart, as John Newton, a hymn writer of the nineteenth century, once said, takes enormous sensitivity and discernment. It does not often occur through "random thoughts" thrown together at the end of a busy week during which the pastor has been doing more "relevant work."

The task of preaching provides the pastor an opportunity to recover the vocation of resident theologian in the community. Here, the pastor needs to become a prayerful thinker and a thinking prayer, and an artist of words for the sake of the Word. Here, creative imagination serves faithful proclamation. Here, weekly listening in conversation with parishioners, literature, biography, television, movies, newspapers, journals, and such forms the sea of concerns, questions, and hopes on which the pastor floats a life-saving, life-engendering, life-enhancing word from the Word of life. Here, the pastor spends much time with the Bible and the tools that promote hermeneutical wisdom. Here, the pastor holds in one hand the book of life and in the other hand the "letters of lives." Here, the pastor lives the prayer of Thomas Aquinas:

> Creator past all telling, you have appointed from the treasures of your wisdom the hierarchies of angels, disposing them in wondrous order above the bright

universe. You we call the true fount of wisdom and the noble origin of all things. Be pleased to shed on the darkness of mind in which I was born, the twofold beam of your light and warmth to dispel my ignorance and sin. You make eloquent the tongues of children. Then instruct my speech and touch my lips with graciousness. Make me keen to understand, quick to learn, able to remember; make me delicate to interpret and ready to speak. Guide my going in and going forward, and lead home my going forth. You are true God and true man, and live for ever and ever. Amen.[15]

The preacher as theologian takes time, preparation, and spiritual insight.

Congregations continually and consistently say, "Send us preachers!" Whatever else they want, they want competent preachers. The question is whether or not congregations will give pastors time to be preachers.

Preaching itself as spoken and heard within a congregation is also a weekly rite of passage. It is a bringing of all the past week's (in some cases month's or year's) struggle with one's humanity, social relationships, vocation, questions, and longings into the presence of the word of the gospel. Here, an intersection takes place between a person's life and Christ's life. Sometimes that intersection is a place of gentle caress; sometimes it is a violent collision. The liminal moment in the mixing of these two stories in a truly gospel sermon will most likely involve the movement from orientation to disorientation to reorientation. This transition is marked by the announcement of the good news in which the parishioner and the congregation, along with the preacher, move to another beginning for another week of the journey.

If the sermon is worthy, it will help to interpret life toward meaning in light of the gospel, and it will address the fundamental theological question by offering a word that gives life, engenders life, and makes life possible.

Prayer

What does it mean to be a "praying church?" Or a "praying pastor?" The obvious answer is a church or a pastor that prays. And don't all churches and pastors do that? Perhaps. In a way.

The problem is that prayer, as a way of life, is one of the most essential but elusive of the spiritual disciplines in the pastoral vocation. It is elusive for several reasons.

- The life of prayer takes time, a commodity conceived to be in short supply by most pastors.
- The life of prayer is not a matter of programming.
- The life of prayer is not a technique that can be easily learned and mastered.
- The life of prayer cannot be measured.
- The life of prayer partakes of the mystical.
- The life of prayer is not about obtaining aims and goals and meeting one's needs.
- The life of prayer is not pragmatic.
- There are not many "teachers" of prayer in the Protestant tradition.

In contrast to the above, the life of prayer is attentiveness to God. It is a mind-set of the Spirit, a habit of being. It is concerned with the knowledge and experience of God and the knowledge and experience of one's own life. The life of prayer moves beyond "knowing about" to knowing and unknowing. It requires humility, tenacity, and honesty. It is emptying; it is filling; it is relational. It involves practicing the presence of God.

In short, prayer involves anchorage, the rooting of one's life and ministry in the mystery of God. That is daunting, and many of us pastors, whether liberal or conservative, progressive or traditional, activists or pietists—it makes not a bit difference—are actually uncomfortable with mystery, unfamiliar with our own inner terrain, unable to give up control, and unsure of our faith. If the functions of our ministries are not manipulable, measurable, and manageable, we are lost and uncertain.

Yet prayer is our lifeline with God, and ministry that is not hidden in God is lost in the world. Prayer becomes the minimum condition of a God-centered ministry. God exists for us when we "pray God's presence," and God exists for those in our pastoral care when we "pray God's presence" for them. This is not to be misunderstood as saying God exists because we pray. But the life of ministry separated from the practice and teaching of prayer is a kind of functional atheism, a God-forgetfulness. Yet the life of prayer is difficult. Life centered in God is a struggle. The practice of prayer and the practice of the presence of God is not perfunctory. It is not result-oriented, even if the results we desire are spiritual. It is therefore easier for the pastor to teach about God than to commune with God. It is easier to pontificate than to pray, easier to rush about parish life than to reside in God, easier to be interrupted for doing good works than to practice uninterrupted patience in prayer. Can you think of anyone's ministry more full of interruptions than Jesus' ministry? Nonetheless, his ministry was anchored in God through constant prayer.

To be a praying church and a praying pastor involves a major reorientation of the pastoral ministry and the life of the congregation to orientation toward God. It is to recover the Hebrew *shema*: "Hear, O Israel: The LORD is our God, the LORD alone. You shall love the LORD your God with all your heart, and with all your soul, and with all your might."[16] To be a praying church and a praying pastor is to struggle against idolatry. It is not speaking about God all the time but being willing to be addressed and taught by God. It is a gathering up of the ins and outs, the loves and hatreds, the fears and hopes, the passions and the apathy, and presenting the "all" that is within us to the "all" that is God. When I speak of prayer, then, as central to the pastoral vocation, what I have in mind is not some super-spiritual, hyper-pious person incessantly jabbering about God and prayer and devotions. I am encouraging pastors to struggle for the time, patience, honesty, self-awareness, and silence required to attend to the mystery of our own humanity in its "everydayishness" in the presence of the Creator, Redeemer, and Sustainer of that humanity.

The life of prayer can also be conceptualized as a rite of passage. Rituals will accompany its practice in both the personal life of the pastor and the corporate praying of the church. While not easily divided in the vocation of prayer, there are the preliminal rites, in which there is enough separation from the immediate to give attention to the eternal (for example, closing a door, lighting a candle, kneeling, taking deep breaths, keeping silence, etc);[17] there is the liminal rite (prayer itself in its varied forms); there are the postliminal rites (for example, easing out of silence, blowing out a candle and watching the smoke rise and disperse, rising to serve, etc.).

Perhaps in prayer as in nothing else there is revelation: Life becomes interpreted toward meaning in light of the gospel. In prayer one comes to see and hear more clearly oneself, one's community, one's world, one's God. And in that seeing and hearing is the word that gives life.

Confession and Absolution

We Protestants do not speak much about confession and absolution other than in the context of the corporate confession of sin and the assurance of pardon in public worship. While corporate confession and the assurance of pardon are clearly public rituals in the liturgy—as they should be—it is my belief that the rite of confession should be recovered in the life of the Protestant church as part of the pastoral vocation and life of the community of faith. I do not mean this in terms of a legalistic requirement, but in terms of an offer of divine help in the incarnational means of gospel speaking.

In the typical Protestant congregation there is conversation, pastoral counseling, generalization in speaking about "our sins," but there is seldom the actual practice of auricular confession— confession to the ear of a confessor. If confession actually takes place, there is seldom the practice of absolution: "By the authority of Christ, I forgive you of your sins." The idea of the sacramental nature of confession has long been abandoned by most Protestant churches and clergy.

The result has been that pastors are left with exercising human therapies rather than the therapy of the word of God. Counseling is not confession. Searching for behavioral alternatives in human neurosis is not absolution. The language of the psychiatrist is not the language of the gospel. This does not mean the pastor is to devalue the place and role of human psychotherapy, psychology, psychiatry, and counseling. Indeed, the pastor should, in many cases, make referrals for psychiatric and psychological therapy. But it does mean that the pastor is to develop clarity about his or her own vocation and not to confuse pastoral counseling with either secular therapy or sacramental confession. Dietrich Bonhoeffer reminds us that before a psychiatrist a person can be a sick person, but before a brother or a sister a person can be a sinner.[18]

I speak of sacramental confession in the historic sense of penance. Penance is a sacrament in which sins committed after baptism are forgiven. It is important that the graces of the gospel are incarnate, made flesh, in the life of the church. This moves the spiritual life from the realm of the purely subjective and ideational to the communal and the concrete. The Christian is not left alone to deal with his or her own sins simply in his or her own mind. Confession and absolution are gifts offered at a time when a person is likely to be his or her own worst enemy. The inner enemy can manifest itself either through self-flagellation and self-despising guilt or through easy dismissal and self-delusion. Through the practice of confession, sin and grace can meet each other, and sin and forgiveness can be objectified.

All this makes sense only if the congregation has been led by the pastor into an understanding of genuine Christian fellowship where the community gathers not just as devout, moral, and good people, but as a fellowship of sinners. It makes sense if the realities of sin and grace have not been psychologized—reduced to psychological categories. It makes sense only if the Christian life is interpreted through the cross and resurrection of Jesus Christ and if the church is understood as a forgiven and forgiving community. The practice of confession and absolution actually contributes to the building of authentic *Christian* community.

"Confess your sins to one another"[19] is an offer of divine help through human agency in the sacramental life of the church. It brings a rhythm of grace into the life of the Christian in which time and place is made to examine and reflect on one's life and in which breakthrough to new life is made possible. As such, confession and absolution is another rite of passage in which the ritual helps the Christian to move from past experiences through change and transformation to a new place in life. The preliminal rites would involve the examining of conscience and the "offering your gift at the altar…"[20] This creates a separation from the past. The liminal rite is in the confession and the absolution. The postliminal rite may involve a form of penance and the new experience of life in forgiveness.

The practice of confession and absolution within the congregation interprets life toward meaning through the cross and resurrection, sin and forgiveness. It centers the life of the church in the very story that created it rather than in psychological and sociological terms. It centers the life of the church in forgiveness and redemption rather than in programs designed to "meet the needs of the people" and worship designed to "satisfy personal tastes." The church can once again speak the word that brings life, engenders life, and makes life possible—forgiveness and freedom.

Suffering

Luther's seventh mark of the church is the cross. It is posited not only as central to the story of Jesus but also in contrast to Christian triumphalism. The choice is between a theology of glory and a theology of the cross. This is a difficult mark for white middle- and upper-middle-class churches in North America. The cultural context of these churches is such that suffering is hidden, denied, repressed, and pushed to the edges. In a culture of success, suffering, brokenness, and failure are taboo. And the church in a culture of success and excess in many ways reflects its culture and bends away from suffering. Yet just beneath the surface of this culture and the church's reflection of it is deep human ache, fear, and fragmentation.[21]

In psychiatrist Irvin Yalom's novel *When Nietzsche Wept*, he speaks of detaching trivial misery from its perch in order to make suffering honest again.[22] The pastor with vocational clarity will recognize this task as part and parcel of vocational integrity. Rather than hiding suffering and running from it, the pastor will help the church engage suffering and find redemption in it. If we are to suffer more than bruised egos, which will put us in touch with nothing that matters, then suffering can put us at great advantage. Remember, the suffering and privation of the desert experience often became the locus for revelation and contact with God.

The pastor is called to be in the front lines of faith and doubt, suffering and sorrow, loneliness and longing, where souls are broken fields, plowed by pain. And, of course, "the front lines" of any action are always on the margins of social order and social acceptance. A great danger for us pastors is to be tamed by cultural definitions of success and institutional desires for security to such an extent that we live in avoidance of suffering and as far away from the margins and the marginalized as we can get. It is difficult to lead a church to the margins and the marginalized from the center of security. It is difficult to speak Christianly in contexts of suffering from a perspective of "happy talk," success-oriented Christianity.

In a world where God's presence is squeezed out, it is extremely difficult to keep attentive to God. In a world where hate and suspicion continue to grow, it is hard to continue to love. In a world marked by pain, it is hard to praise. In a world of injustice and tragedy, it is hard to give thanks. How hard it is in Godforsakenness to call on God. Yet this is exactly the word of Jesus from the cross.[23] Vocational clarity in the pastorate in regard to suffering is especially critical in times when suffering, adversity, and affliction come to the pastor's own life, which they inevitably will. Can the pastor at that point continue to call on the God of Godforsakenness? Can the pastor continue to believe, continue to love, continue to hope, continue to give thanks? It is only possible for the pastor whose formation has taken shape through attention to the gospel story, whose weekly path leads to and from the eucharistic table of participation in the body and blood of Christ, and whose servanthood is defined by the Suffering Servant of God. God's Suffering Servant brings healing not through his power, slickness, technique, gimmickry, and success, but through his wounds.[24]

The ultimate rite of passage is from death to life. For the pastor this involves walking the *via dolorosa* with the people in his or her pastoral care. This "way of tears" leads into the quiet, lonely, and hidden places of suffering, and for us all finally into the "valley of the shadow." But, as Nietzsche said, "Only where there are graves is there resurrection." And this is the word that gives life.

Healing Fountains

As I have said, vocational confusion leads to functional maceration of the pastor as the pastor lives by reactive response to the crises and claims of the people. Confusion begets confusion within the life of the congregation. On the other hand, vocational clarity leads to functional focus in pastoral tasks. Faithful commitment to the doing of these tasks reinforces the pastor's vocational clarity, giving ontological integrity to the pastor's life and work. Ritualizing the marks of the church centers the pastoral life in worship for the sake of the worshiping community. The healing fountains are baptism, preaching, eucharist, prayer, confession and absolution, and engagement of suffering.

But the pastor and the church are not always gathered in worship. They are also dispersed in worship—in the mission of the church in the world. This is the "liturgy after the liturgy." What of pastoral clarity in the day-to-day running of the church? This is where the tapestry of liturgy in the pastor's life often becomes unraveled. It is to this issue that we now turn.

CHAPTER 9

The Pastor with the People

How shall I live among this people who have called me to serve as their pastor? Nikos Katzanzakis' words are not far removed from pastoral realities. "Our love for each other is rough and ready, we sit at the same table, we drink the same wine in this low tavern of life." People are so much alike and yet so different. They are haunted or blessed, or both, from all their yesterdays. They seek some kind of tomorrow. They are so gifted, yet so wounded. They are not unlike their pastor in all these ways. We do sit at the same table. We do drink the same wine in this low tavern of life.

Until now we have been reflecting on what might be called the "set lectionary" of pastoral life: ordination vows taken, promises made, boundaries marked off, job descriptions focused, identifying marks named, and vocational identity clarified by the past history and living tradition of the church and the gospel it preaches. We now move to the "existential lectionary" of the pastoral life: the roughness and the readiness of it all. This includes the uniqueness of experience, the particularities of each human story, the specific social complexities of time and circumstance. It gets rowdy in this low tavern!

Pastoral work is not factory work. It is not assembly line work. Its concerns are not with making widgets. It is art and craft, not mechanization and mass production. It involves creativity more than engineering. It is a person-making, community-creating work. And that kind of work can only be done with great attention to the materials being used and the minute details of construction. My wife is a woodworker, and whatever she makes, she makes with enormous attention to the details of size, shape, fit, stress, structure, quality, and finish. No art can be rushed; nor can the art of care and cure of souls.

How shall I live among this people who have called me to serve as their pastor? How shall I live in such a way as to keep vocational clarity intact and response to the particularity of human need in sight? How can I pay attention to the details of both without losing my own personhood?

How Shall I Live?...

1. In Solidarity

Solidarity means unity of sympathies and interests. It means camaraderie. It means to take one's place alongside of and to stand with. It will serve the pastor well in the pastoral vocation to be among the people in a spirit of solidarity. The pastor is neither superior nor inferior within the community of believers. Augustine said of his bishopric and his life among the people, "For you I am a bishop, but with you I am a Christian. The first is an office accepted; the second is a gift received. One is danger; the other is safety. If I am happier to be redeemed with you, then I shall, as the Lord commanded, be more fully your servant."[1] Solidarity with the people is a means to servanthood. Vocational clarity in regard to the pastoral office is a means to faithfulness. One can practice solidarity without abdicating the responsibilities of the pastoral office. Both serve the building up of a community that is Christian.

Living among the people of God in solidarity addresses the issue of pastoral authority. We are living in a time when the very concept of authority is suspect, even rejected, and with good reason. One cannot discuss the meaning of authority without discussing the use of power.

It has been the misuse and abuse of power that, among other things, has led to the widespread rejection of authority. The concern with power and its use within the church and by the church was addressed in chapter 5. Suffice it to say here that authoritarianism simply will not be considered as sufficient reason for anything.

However, if authority essentially means "to author," then the stance of pastoral authority in the congregation is the mutual "authoring" of the life of the community. The pastor is a part of that community, not a separate, detached, authoritarian presence. At the same time, as minister of word and sacrament, as community theologian, the pastor is not to abandon the responsibility of the vocation in the name of solidarity. Solidarity is to offer the gifts, the training, and the responsibilities accepted in the vocation to the community in order to help them become mutual interpreters of texts and co-authors of congregational life. In practical terms this would mean the teaching role of the pastor would not be based on methods of indoctrination. This is what Paulo Friere called the "banking method of education."[2] Rather, effective pastoral teaching grows out of mutual exploration in which members of the congregation become the subjects of their own learning. Companionship and conversation become the mode of solidarity in which pastor and people together learn and live the faith with special attention to all gifts present and all contexts addressed.

Living among the people in solidarity becomes a matter of interrelatedness and interdependence. It protects the pastor from the pride of independence and the people from roles of dependency. Solidarity with pastoral clarity allows the pastor to do his or her own work while empowering the laity to be the church and do their own work. Growth and vitality occur for pastor and people alike through genuine relationship. Carl Rogers's point about client-centered therapy applies as well to the concept of solidarity in pastoral life among the people: "I cannot be of help by means of any intellectual or training procedure. No approach which relies upon knowledge, upon training, upon the acceptance of something *taught,* is of any use. The failure of any such approach through the intellect has forced me to recognize that change appears to come about through *experience in a relationship.*"[3] Rogers's statement should not be taken to mean anti-intellectualism. It does mean that reliance on technique or dogmatism or the requiring of intellectual assent or keeping human exchange only at the level of ideas as a means to growth, maturity, and transformation will not work. Such approaches may lead to control but not to personal and communal growth. Solidarity with the people cultivates in the congregation what Roy SteinhoffSmith has called the "mutuality of care."[4]

Solidarity thus involves the sharing of one's own story, one's own humanity, and one's own faith journey in the community of faith. It involves receiving as well as giving in this mutuality of care. This challenges the misguided promotion of "aloofness" and the rejection of pastoral friendship within the congregation as a means of protecting professional boundaries, which has been advocated over the past fifteen years and recommended in many judicatory training sessions on clergy ethics. Boundaries are clearly important,[5] but not at the expense of the integrity of *koinonia* and the mutuality of care in the friendship of Jesus.

2. With Perspective

Solidarity with the people of God requires not only empathetic involvement, but *empathetic involvement that includes the pastoral perspective.* It is the loss of perspective, not the denial of relationships, that endangers clarity in the pastoral vocation. The pastor brings authenticity to his or her congregational involvement not by abdicating the pastoral role, but precisely by offering the gifts, training, and clarity of the vocation to the community. The perspective of the pastor is theological and liturgical: attentiveness to God, the story of the gospel, the life of the spirit, the history of the tradition, and the content of the faith. The church is a theological community, and it is with this perspective that the theological pastor enters community life. Without the gift of the theological voice, a voice that shapes the community of grace in faith and for the love and worship of God, a key ingredient to Christian community is missing.

Some years ago a British film was released entitled *Wetherby.* It didn't get much public notice. It was one of those dark, "talky," British dramas without a single chase scene! It tells the story of a stranger who arrives at a cottage along with another couple for a dinner party. The host assumes the couple brought the stranger, and the couple assumes the host had invited the stranger. An evening of conversation ensues about life and its proclivities—love, faith, philosophy, psychology, violence, alienation, education. During the course of the conversation the stranger says, "Well, I don't know. I only know goodness and anger and revenge and evil and desire. These seem to me to be far better words than neurosis and psychology and paranoia. These old words...These good old words. They have a sort of conviction which all this modern apparatus of language now lacks. We bury these words, these simple feelings. We bury them deep. And all the building over that constitutes this century will not wish these feelings away." The other guest replies, "Well, ole boy, you'll have to say what you really mean by that. Define your terms." The stranger says, "They don't need defining. If you can't feel them, you might as well be dead."

There are some "good old words." There are words central to the gospel. All the building over that constitutes this past century cannot wish these words away if Christian identity is to remain within the Christian congregation. The pastor with vocational clarity lives among the people with a perspective.

3. Out of Integrity

Living among the people out of integrity means not only living with honesty and steadfastness but also living with a sense of wholeness and integration. What the pastor does and who the pastor is are integrated, and dependably so, for the sake of the community. Frederick Buechner speaks to the issue of pastoral integrity, in one way or another, in almost all his writings. But he especially does so in *Telling Secrets*[6] and *Telling the Truth: The Gospel as Tragedy, Comedy and Fairy Tale.*[7] He draws attention to the relationship of the pastor's faith with the pastor's preaching. He makes the distinction between giving lectures and preaching sermons. He shows the difference between analyzing ideas and gospel proclamation. He commends preaching in which the faith the preacher is laying before the community is the faith that is being drawn out of the raw stuff of the preacher's own life. He believes a person attending divinity school while not believing in divinity is a peculiarly depressing form of bankruptcy. He ponders whether one who ignores the ordination vows would have the courage to turn in the ordination certificate.

The integration of the pastor's office with the pastor's personhood, with integrity, and then living among the people with that sense of cohesion, is a reflection of the doctrine of the incarnation. Pastoral care becomes care incarnate in bodily presence rather than advice giving and theoretical insight. Faith is shared person-to-person rather than *persona*-to-*persona*. Living out of this integrity with the people results in a face-to-face meeting, not a face-to-mask or a face-to-role meeting. This kind of authenticity does not mean the pastor is a paragon of virtue with no doubt, no sins, no struggles, no darkness, no grief, no humanity! Quite the opposite. It is a way of being in oneself and with the other that makes possible the other's bringing his or her own personhood, with all its complexities, to God and the journey of faith. Catholic writer Louis Evely has said,

> Since people don't have the courage to mature unless someone has faith in them, we have to reach those we meet at the level where they stopped developing, where they were given up as hopeless, and so withdrew into themselves and began to secrete a protective shell because they thought they were alone and no one cared. They have to know they're loved very deeply and very boldly before

they dare appear humble and kind, affectionate, sincere and vulnerable.[8]

Genuine pastoral relationships cannot occur through the "protective pastoral shells" with which we surround ourselves. In the integrity of the mutuality of care, nothing authentic and at the deepest level of the heart can occur when we dance shell-to-shell. We must dance face-to-face. The "putting off of the old person" (protective shell) in the transforming presence of Jesus is not enhanced by a pastor whose life among the people is lived in a protective shell.

4. Through Approachability

This brings us to living among the people through approachability. One of the remarkable things about the ministry of Jesus was his approachability. The lepers, the blind, the publicans, the Pharisees, the teachers, the women, the rich, the poor, and the peasant all seemed to be able to come into his presence and to be given his presence and attention.

Approachability, however, does not mean the giving up of all privacy and the practice of solitude. In the *Regula Pastorum* presented in chapter 6, I suggested the pastor should strive to divide his or her time as equally as possible between being a servant of the Word and a servant of the people. Time for prayer, study, and reflection must be protected.

But when one is among the people, it is important to be approachable. We make ourselves unapproachable in a number of ways. Perhaps the most common is to hide behind our busyness and our preoccupations. As moving targets we are hard to hit! Our always being on the run may be a matter of running away from more than running toward. The question of availability will be discussed with reference to community building in a later chapter. But without a slower pace on our part, it is difficult for people to approach us. Another barrier to approachability is to give off an air of such importance that no one would dare to interrupt us. I had a beloved professor at Union Theological Seminary who placed this sign on his study door: "Please knock. I would hate to think I lived my life without disturbing anyone." Pastors should live their lives with this sign on the door of their hearts: "Please knock." An air of "hard piety" can also make us unapproachable. If there is such a thing as "easy virtue," there is also such a thing as "hard righteousness." Unfortunately, we can live in such a way as to make people think, "I can't talk to him/her about *that*."

Approachability is part of what it means to be a priest, a bridge. It is to look for ways to make access possible. Making love, making believe, and creating hope—all central to the pastoral vocation— require a leisurely pace, a place of connection and touch, and a period of time filled with patient possibility.

5. By Tenacity

Life among the people can be trying, tiring, and exceedingly frustrating! A resolve to live with a certain tenacity is an important quality for the pastor among the people. It is the willingness to hold on to, to not let go of, people. It involves being able to stick to a relationship. Therefore, it requires the gift of patience. The word *patience* comes from the Latin "to endure or to suffer." Paul's mandate to "bear one another's burdens, and in this way you will fulfill the law of Christ" is not simply a matter of carrying this or that difficulty, but suffering a person's presence, suffering the person himself/herself.

Being among the people with tenacity is one of the reasons there is an eschatological dimension to the exercise of the pastoral vocation. Not all things can be fixed; not all relationships can be healed; not all sufferings can be removed. Nothing—no one and no relationship—comes to complete fulfillment in this life. Reinhold Niebuhr remains our best teacher here: "Nothing worth doing is completed in one lifetime. Therefore we must be saved by hope. Nothing true and beautiful makes complete sense in any context of history. Therefore we must be saved by faith. Nothing we do, no matter how virtuous, can be accomplished alone. Therefore we are saved by love."[9] Tenacity is required to bear adversity in faith and to learn from it. The pastor must live with tenacious hope, knowing that most pastoral victories remain hidden until the day of Christ.

This is the point of a reflection by Oscar Romero shortly before he was martyred in March of 1980. It poignantly speaks to the issue of tenacity in a long faithfulness of ministry anchored in eschatological hope:

It helps, now and then, to step back and take the long view. The kingdom is not only beyond our efforts, it is even beyond our vision. We accomplish in our lifetime only a tiny fraction of the magnificent enterprise that is God's work. Nothing we do is complete, which is another way of saying that the kingdom lies beyond us. No statement says all that could be said. No prayer fully expresses our faith. No confession brings perfection. No pastoral visit brings wholeness. No program accomplishes the church's mission. No set of goals and objectives includes everything. This is what we are about: We plant seeds that one day will grow. We water seeds already planted, knowing that they hold future promise. We lay foundations that will need further development. We provide yeast that produces effects beyond our capabilities. We cannot do everything, and there is a sense of liberation in realizing that. This enables us to do something, and to do it very well. It may be incomplete, but it is a beginning, a step along the way, an opportunity for God's grace to enter and do the rest. We may never see the end results, but that is the difference between the master builder and the worker. We are workers, not master builders, ministers, not messiahs. We are prophets of a future not our own."[10]

6. With Passion

The opposite of love is not hate; it is apathy. It is to live without passion, without feeling, and without fervor. We have already explored the nature of the God who calls to Christian ministry: God is the passionate and vulnerable God of the gospel. The minister of word and sacrament is called to live out of that call. The core narrative of that word and sacrament is called "the passion"—the suffering love of Christ. The life and death of Jesus Christ reveals a God who suffers for, with, and in people. Jesus invites us into a community of passion with God and others; thus, the pastor is called to live a passionate life among the people.

To be passionate is to be moved, to be acted on, to be vulnerable. It is to live life as a love letter, putting into pastoral work, as you would put into a love letter, all the feeling, excitement, care, hope, and commitment of your life. Passion in the pastoral life partakes of the world of dreams and visions. There is something of the madness of being in love in the pastoral vocation. It is lived in the hope that what results is not simply institutional growth but, by grace, new life, new community, and new social realities. Indeed, it is to provoke dreams of new communities, new relationships, and new worlds beyond the worlds that do not make room for life, love, freedom, and justice. It is to live among the people toward a world for which our hearts ache and our spirits long.

Such ministry cannot occur without passion or compassion. A passionless gospel and a passionless ministry are oxymorons.

But it really is a bit mad to spend one's life passionately listening for God, praying to God, arguing with God for the sake of your people, wrestling with your people for the sake of God, waiting for God, enduring the silence of God, speaking of God, and trying day and night to keep the world open for the possibility of God. Why would anyone get involved in this passionate madness? The only reason I know is because of this thing called vocation. Because somewhere back there we have eaten bread and found *cum panis*—with bread we found companionship, relationship, and a love that will not let us go. We have "eaten the scroll" and cannot forget. We have seen and dreamed and heard and tasted—and life can never be the same again. We have fallen in love, and the only way to live that love out among the people is with passion.

But wherever love is the deepest, pain is the sharpest. Our struggle as pastors is to keep from falling out of love as we live life among the people, enduring the suffering that love inevitably brings. "Not to feel" becomes a self-protective mechanism. And what begins as a defense mechanism can become habitual apathy. Pastors often begin with little experience and lots of enthusiasm. They often end with lots of experience and little enthusiasm. Attending to the pastoral passion for life will be a subject of chapter 12, lest we become examples of Nietzsche's quip, "You will have to look more redeemed if I am to believe in your Redeemer."[11]

The Four Historic Functions of Pastoral Care

Living among the people in solidarity, with perspective, out of integrity, through approachability, by tenacity, and with passion will enhance the pastor's means of fulfilling the four historic functions of pastoral care.[12] In a time of desert hearts, when so much emphasis continues to be placed on building successful churches, church growth, institutional survival, and church programming to meet the needs of the people, a brief reminder of these simple honesties of the care and cure of souls is important. It is in and through these functions that the caravan community can find the living fountains.

1. The Ministry of Healing

All people are wounded, broken, and bent out of shape in some way or another. All of us are diseased and dis-eased. The Greek word for healing means wholeness, and it is used in connection with both physical and spiritual health and is often connected with salvation. The ministry of Jesus was a ministry of healing. While his practice of healing reflected in many ways the practice of the ancient "medical schools" in the Aesculapius, there was also a distinct difference. As was the case with his eating habits, he healed indiscriminately and promiscuously. There was no requirement of either purity or payment.

In the contemporary world healing has largely been relegated to the medical professions. But even here there is a recognition of treating the whole person, and there has been a growing role in the medical community for chaplains, spiritual directors, and hospices. Healing, of course, belongs in the province of the medical profession. But it also belongs in the province of the church and the practice of pastoral care. This pastoral function is committed to healing the wounds in human existence. Pastoral care attends to the cure of souls.

2. The Ministry of Sustaining

The ministry of sustaining involves the pastoral function of helping hurting persons endure and transcend circumstances in which restoration or healing is virtually impossible. Not everything can be fixed, every problem overcome, every tragedy reversed. There is death. There is loss. There is irrefragable brokenness. Humpty Dumpty cannot be put back together again. Many of the final discourses of Jesus in John's gospel (his own pastoral speaking) were focused on sustaining the disciples through the dark ravine. The ministry of sustaining helps gather the fragments of life, helps hold the line against further loss, is patient in grief, is faithful in hope. Here, the pastor holds a hand rather than gives an answer. Holding the hand is the connection with life and the first act of gently leading a person back to life either on a new basis or in a different form. In the end, offering presence becomes the most important act of mercy.

3. The Ministry of Guiding

Pastoral work is a work of guiding. How critical this is in the desert experience. The act of guiding others flows out of that pastoral willingness to be guided oneself, to be taught by God. Otherwise, as Jesus said, "If the blind lead the blind, both will fall into the ditch."[13] Christian guidance is based on the recognition that Jesus is the way, as well as the truth and the life. To guide in the way is to walk in the way. Guidance is the task of helping people to find their way in the world. It is the ministry of wisdom. Surely pastoral work is to shape the theological community in such a way as to make the Christian community that place where people can find guidance for life, where wisdom is nurtured, and where spiritual light shines in the darkness.

4. The Ministry of Reconciliation

Reconciliation is the ministry of bridge-building, connection-making, fence-mending, peace-promoting, harmony-restoring presence. It is the ministry and the message we have been given.[14] Through the ministry of reconciliation the pastor deals with the alienation that exists within the soul of a person, between a person and other persons, and between a person and God. This is gospel work at its heart.

These historic functions of pastoral care are merely the reflections of God's own work. For God is the healer of wounds, the sustainer of our lives, the guide to abundant life, and the reconciler of all that is separated. Pastors do well to live in the constant reminder, in the words of the apostle Paul, that we are the clay jars that carry the treasure.[15] The treasure is not us. The power is not ours. The ministry and its results are left in the hands of God, and this is both humbling and freeing. If we do our work well in performing these functions among the people, with clarity and focus, everything else will take care of itself—mission, growth, evangelism, fellowship, communion, renewal.

CHAPTER 10

The Pastor and Christian Community

Is the church important anymore? In an age of individualism, expressed in religious terms by the rising quest for "individual spiritualities" and in secular terms by the quest for "personal fulfillment," one might think not. To hear some pastors talk, the church is even conceived as the enemy of anything authentically Christian.

To be sure, the church has much to answer for, and we pastors perhaps even more. I have already discussed the shadow side of the church's history. Yet the quest for meaningful community persists both inside and outside the church. The question is, Why is the formation of authentic Christian community so elusive in North American culture? "Community" is a fashionable issue, but moving beyond an understanding and practice of church that has more meaning than as a place to attend is another matter. The development of a group of people in a socially comfortable situation built on the famed "homogeneity" made popular by the church growth movement is not necessarily a *Christian* community.

Hans Kung warns that the church can become an agglomeration of individual Christians, each living his or her own life, but this can scarcely be called a church, a congregation, a community.[1] George Lindbeck has argued fiercely for the importance of Christian community in today's world. What is called for even in ecumenical work is the

> reconstituting of Christian community and unity from, so
> to speak, the ground up...This focus on building Christian

115

community will seem outrageous to some in view of the world's needs, but it is a strength for those who see the weakening of communal commitments and loyalties as modernity's fundamental disease. Perhaps no greater contribution to peace, justice and the environment is possible than that provided by the existence of intercontinental and interconfessional communal networks such as the churches are to some extent, and can become more fully, if God wills.[2]

Douglas John Hall lists the search for meaningful community as one of the most important worldly quests of our time.[3]

Vocational clarity can help the pastor address this issue because it points the pastor to what he or she ought to be doing. The pastor as program director, CEO, therapist, change agent, and facilitator of a "church for everyone's tastes" is hardly conducive to the building of Christian community. The pastor as minister of word and sacrament, who is the community theologian for the theological community, is. One of the reasons community is elusive in the North American church, and the one that concerns us in this conversation, is that pastors have been unclear on their vocation, and the church has been unclear on its identity. With vocational clarity, the pastor can once again become an artist of community.

What Is Needed?

1. A New Sanctification of Time

Sanctification is to make holy. The sanctification of time is to declare or render time conducive to holiness. It is to bless time and purify it, to set it apart for holy use. This may seem a strange beginning for the building of Christian community. However, a chief sin of North American culture in relationship to time is the over-busyness with which we live. What is true of the culture is true of the church, and what is true of the church is true of pastors. We are all too busy to be Christian! We are too busy to create community!

The sanctification of time is to bring to life within the community of faith the rhythms of grace in which time is measured not by how every minute is filled, but by how every moment is kept. The sanctification of time attends not to the speed at which it is lived, but to the meaning it is given. Sanctified time is timely—appropriate. Living in sanctified time is to yield *chronos* (the time of the clock and the calendar) to *kairos* (the time of God's moment, pregnant with possibilities). To use Paul Tillich's term, it is to begin to live in the eternal now of God's presence.

As attention is given to the sanctification of time, the pastor's work will involve leading the congregation into the daily, weekly, and monthly times and seasons of the Christian year. Life in the community will begin to follow the time flow of the story that shapes its life. But above all, the pastor will call for cessation of busyness—including religious busyness—those activities in the church designed to keep people occupied. The last thing people need is something else to *do*! The pastoral call for the cessation of busyness will be accompanied by the call to Sabbath time.[4] This call from busyness to Sabbath, from action to rest, will be a sign within the community that those who follow Christ in the world do not find their identity in being producers and consumers. Without a new commitment to the sanctification of time, no community is really possible.

2. Intentional Focus

Clarity in the pastor's life helps bring clarity to congregational life. As we have seen, focus is an avenue to clarity. If congregations are to become more than an agglomeration of individuals dipping into the church from their privatized and over-busy lives, focus on community will need to become a priority. The focus needs to move from programs to people. "Weeping with those who weep and rejoicing with those who rejoice" is a daily way of living, not an occasional virtue. Two Quakers were sitting in a train station, and one asked the other, "Do you love me?" "Of course, I love you," came the reply. "But how can you love me if you do not know what is troubling me?" People cannot hug programs. Program verbs are promote, administer, indoctrinate, enroll, succeed, fail, proselytize. Community verbs are serve, grow, discover, befriend, sojourn, suffer, teach, preach, overcome, learn, celebrate. Inherited loyalties, denominational allegiance, and geographical convenience are no longer very influential motivators for involvement in a church. They certainly aren't central in people's minds in their quest for understanding, belonging, and the experience of meaningful community. Many long-term church leaders still believe that the way to motivate people is through challenge and the call for greater commitment. The fact is, the rank and file, whether churched or unchurched, are motivated by the desire for community and the need for compassion.

A program-focused church is organized around functions. Activities are programmed for the people. The pastor then sets out to enlist people to work in the programs when they are already over-enlisted. Volunteer work can be done in many sectors of the society. A people-focused church is organized around relationships. This promotes community. A caring church is a relational church; this focus grows out of the gospel because the gospel is a relational gospel from beginning to end.

The focus of the pastor and the people in a caring church is attentiveness. The lack of attention people feel is poignantly put in Lamentations 1:12 and could be inscribed on many a desert heart in the contemporary world: "Is it nothing to you, all you who pass by? Look and see if there is any sorrow like my sorrow, which was brought upon me." Because our culture is one in which suffering is hidden, the sufferer becomes invisible. It is no wonder the gospel is filled with the admonition to "have eyes that see and ears that hear." It is doubtful that one can see or hear God, if one cannot see or hear the sister or brother right next to one or the neighbor just down the street. Attentiveness is the *sine qua non* of Christian community—attention to God through Jesus Christ and attention to "the least of these" in whom Christ dwells.[5]

The word *care* is from the old English and old high-German word meaning "lament." The book of Lamentations to which I just referred could be called the "Book of Paying Attention." Care means a painstaking and watchful attention. It was at the center of the ministry of Jesus, and the gospel says again and again, "He was moved with compassion." This "mutual-feeling" was also at the heart of the life of the earliest Christian communities.

3. Availability

The sanctification of time and the intentional focus, which are essential to creating authentic Christian community, are expressed through the grace of availability. Antoine de Saint-Exupéry pictures the practice of this grace again and again in his classic *The Little Prince*. One passage encapsulates the meaning of availability beautifully.

The fox gazed at the little prince for a long time. "Please tame me," he said.

"I want to very much," the little prince replied. "But I have not much time. I have friends to discover, and a great many things to understand."

"One only understands the things one tames," said the fox. "Men have no more time to understand anything. They buy things already made at the shops. But there is no shop where one can buy friendship, and so men have no friends any more. If you want a friend, tame me."

"What must I do to tame you?" asked the little prince.

"You must be very patient," replied the fox. "First you sit down at a little distance from me—like that—in the grass. I shall look at you out of the corner of my eye, and you will say nothing...But you will sit a little closer to me every day."[6]

"Sitting a little closer each day" is the grace of availability. The caring church, the church of being and becoming community, holds the grace of availability high on its list of values—how we want to be with each other as we live out our mission toward the vision we have articulated. This moves the focus to doing less, that we might become more to each other and to the stranger.

4. Vulnerability

I have heard it said that the church can hurt you and heal you in the same day. Most of us can testify to that reality in our own experience. To those who resist participation in the church because of its fallacies, foibles, and hypocrisy, I usually say, "If you find a perfect church, don't join it. You'll ruin it."

On the other hand, if you find a vulnerable church, a church in which the pastor and people are vulnerable with one another, it is a good place to be. Vulnerability is one of the things that makes us truly human. And in the truly human church that confesses a fully human Lord, it is vulnerability that makes mutual care a reality. Vulnerability was a hallmark of the ministry of Jesus and will be a hallmark of an authentic community of Jesus movement people.

Of course, passion and love are at the heart of vulnerability. The word itself means "wound," and we are reminded that it is by our Lord's wounds that we are healed. The deeper the love with which one lives, the more profound the hurts and anguishes of life. There is a church in the city near where I minister that calls itself "The Happy Church." We may recoil at the crassness of such a designation for a people who gather in the name of the Suffering Servant, the man of tears, the crucified God. Yet happiness may be an unstated goal in many of our churches that have not learned the difference between happiness and a deep-seated spiritual joy.

The connection between love and suffering is beautifully put by C. S. Lewis in *The Four Loves*.

> To love at all is to be vulnerable. Love anything and your heart will certainly be wrung and possibly be broken. If you want to make sure of keeping it intact, you must give your heart to no one, not even to an animal. Wrap it carefully round with hobbies and little luxuries; avoid all entanglements; lock it up safe in the casket—safe, dark, motionless, airless—it will change. It will not be broken; it will become unbreakable, impenetrable, irredeemable. The alternative to tragedy, or at least to the risk of tragedy, is damnation. The only place outside of Heaven where you can be perfectly safe from all dangers and perturbations of love is Hell. [7]

Without being vulnerable, without the ability to be open to one's own suffering, there seems little likelihood of the possibility of genuine Christian community existing in terms of a caring church. Douglas John Hall, in one of the best books ever written on suffering and faith, fears that we are living in a culture that has lost the capacity to suffer.[8] He believes this has resulted in the inability of people to accept and articulate their own suffering, the inability to enter imaginatively into the suffering of others, and the search for an enemy outside oneself on whom to place blame. This description is what I mean by the hiddenness of suffering in our society and the avoidance of suffering in many of our churches. Hall argues for the need for forums in which suffering can be expressed and explored for redemptive purposes. He points to an example of this in the post-war German novel of Gunther Grass, *The Tin Drum*.

> For it is not true that when the heart is full the eyes necessarily overflow, some people can never manage it, especially in our century, which in spite of all the suffering and sorrow will surely come to be known as the tearless century. It was this drought, this tearlessness that brought those who could afford it to Schmuh's Onion Cellar, where the host handed them a little chopping board—pig or fish— a paring knife for eighty pfennigs, and for twelve marks an ordinary field-, garden-, kitchen-variety onion, and induced them to cut their onions smaller and smaller until the juice—what did the onion juice do? It did what the

world and the sorrows of the world could not do: it brought forth a round, human tear. It made them cry.[9]

The church as a community of the vulnerable (a community where the cross is present, in Luther's terms) could become a true community because it lives where the place of love resides. The pastor's vocational attention, focused in the theology of the cross rather than the theology of glory, can make room for suffering within the community and can bring to light the emotionally and spiritually draining efforts to repress the suffering we know we endure but are afraid to face.

5. Storytelling

I have said earlier in our conversation that faith is shared person-to-person rather than *persona*-to-*persona*. Yet this is hard to achieve in the church when our relationships are maintained at a surface level. Pastoral clarity that focuses itself in the story of the gospel, a story of those Jesus gathered together and around himself in a journey of faith, will help the pastor develop authentic community in the congregation. The focus on gospel "as story" will help shape the church into a community of storytellers. A community that tells truthful stories both grows out of and contributes to availability and vulnerability. It takes time, but it creates a community that becomes personal without being private. It contributes to community building because personal stories become the raw data of theological reflection in a theological community. And it brings awareness that the community itself is writing a story together. This in itself will contribute to the process of discovering authentic images that create an *esprit de corps* that militates against malaise, boredom, and inauthenticity.

Storytelling as a way of being with one another within the community serves the purpose of the formation of both personal identity and congregational identity. It helps the church understand who it is in order to become what it might become. It does so in this way: All storytelling involves recovery, reinterpretation, and reentry. The community and the persons within the community can recover the stories of their lives. But there is no such thing as uninterpreted experience. The process of conversion involves the reinterpretation of one's story in light of the gospel story. From that reinterpretation one can move to reentry into the living of life with more clarity, forgiveness, and grace. It helps make life open-ended. This is true both for individual stories and for the story of the congregation. It combines within the theological community the question of truth with the question of truthfulness, thus contributing to authentic Christian community and personal Christian identity.

Community building grows out of the sanctification of time, intentional focus, availability, vulnerability, and storytelling. Within these dynamics, lonely desert hearts find the living fountains of community. Again, pastoral vocational clarity in these ways of forming community will contribute to ecclesial identity and the empowering of the laity in being the church.

CHAPTER 11

The Pastor as Leader and Administrator

Visit any bookshop or open any batch of mail that comes across a pastor's desk, and you will realize there is a glut of materials and seminars being offered on leadership—church leadership, business leadership, educational leadership, volunteer leadership, team leadership, and on the list could go. The point of our conversation in this chapter is not to focus on the techniques of leadership, but to keep us as pastors attentive to leading in a manner coherent with all that we have been saying about vocational clarity. There is no doubt that good leadership is needed in the church. The problem arises when pastors operate more out of leadership theory applied to church needs than out of pastoral clarity applied to leadership needs. Once again, the area of leadership and administration become technique-oriented rather than theologically grounded.

Leadership and administration are not the same, but they are related. My *Oxford Dictionary* defines leadership in the following ways: to show the way by going first; to precede; to guide by the hand; to cause to live or experience. The Old English word for lead is *laedan*, from *lad*, the way. My dictionary defines *administration* in the following ways: to govern; to manage as a steward. It is from the Latin *ad* (to) *ministrare* (minister). The etymology and actual meanings of these words help to define leadership and administration in the pastoral vocation with theological clarity. Leadership and administration for the pastor should not be reduced to running the church office, organizing programs, and engaging in institutional management. Congregations may think they are paying you to do these things, but pastoral clarity about leadership and administration will itself help bring a deeper understanding of ecclesiology to members of the community. It will help empower their own leadership and administrative gifts in actually being the church. In this way the pastor can fulfill his or her responsibilities to the ordination vow of attending to "order" within the church. Attending to matters of "order" does not involve ordering, bossing, manipulating, planning everything that happens, and begging for volunteer involvement for the "running" of the church. It does involve the ministries of leadership and administration, properly defined and clearly executed, within the context of community building and the mutuality of care.

Let us begin with the matter of administration. Although there are some pastors who enjoy church administration, it has been my experience that most are groaning under the weight of administrative duties. So much time is given to administration that no time is left for leadership. This is partially due to the lack of vocational clarity. Administration then grows unchecked and ends up controlling the pastor rather than the pastor controlling it. Bringing vocational clarity to the task of administration will transform it from being a pastoral prison to a pastoral possibility. When it is recognized as a gift of the Spirit and a task in the church appointed by God[1]—a task different from that of teacher, prophet, and evangelist—administration can serve the pastor and people alike rather than pastors becoming slaves to it and the people becoming bored by it!

What can bring vocational clarity to the pastor's administrative tasks? The pastor's vocation is a matter of identity. This identity is focused in being a minister of word and sacrament. The pastor lives that identity by engaging the disciplines that support the identity. It is in keeping to this clarity that the pastor serves God and the people. Part of serving the people is attending to "order," but this is a task rather than a fundamental identity. A disturbing conversation between Jesus and the disciples on the way up to Jerusalem, shortly before the beginning of the Passion Week, is enlightening in regard to the difference between identity and function or task.[2] James and John request to be seated at the Lord's right and left hands in his time of glory. What better positions of administration and the exercise of rule and power could be sought? Jesus turns the conversation from position and function, which he says are not his to grant, to the center from which one lives—to the question of who one is. "Are you able to drink the cup that I drink, or be baptized with the baptism that I am baptized with?" (Mark 10:38). He then launches into his teaching on servanthood. In the realm of the Gentiles, rule (governings) is exercised by power and authority. This is not the way it is to be in the Jesus community. Governings is done by service.

Governings *(kubernaseis)* is the word used in 1 Corinthians 12 for the gift of administration. As we have seen, it means to manage as a steward, and in Latin it means to serve or to minister. This comes very close to the way Jesus turns the conversation in the passage in Mark 10. Governings, or administration, in the community of faith is not through the exercise of power but through the act of service. Administration is service to the community, not running everything in the community.

The best definition I have seen of church administration that is in keeping with the pastor as resident theologian comes from Alvin J. Lindgren. "Powerful church administration is the involvement of the church in the discovery of her nature and mission and in moving in a coherent and comprehensive manner toward providing such experiences as will enable the church to utilize all her resources and personnel in the fulfillment of her mission in making known God's love for all people."[3] Appropriate administrative work in the pastoral vocation is informed and shaped by the nature of the pastor's leadership. Our dictionary definitions of leadership flow directly into and serve this definition of administration. Leadership entails involvement—to show the way by going first. Leadership involves connection and community—to guide by the hand. Leadership entails "life affirming" actions—to cause to live or experience. Pastoral leadership thus involves the willingness of the pastor first to "be led" into and to "experience" the life-giving way of the gospel and life-engendering presence of the Holy Spirit. Seeing and experiencing "the way" entails vision. Note how these definitions of leadership reflect Lindgrin's definition of church administration: involvement, connection, community, movement *(lad*, "the way"), and vision.

The pastor does not exist in the Christian community to "do the work of the community." The pastor is present to help the Christian community do its work. It can only do its work well if the pastor does the pastoral work well and leaves the work of the people to the people. The pastor's work in administration can best be understood through using the image of hospitality.

The pastor invites the people into, sets the table for, and convenes the conversation for the administrative work. The pastor's contribution to administrative work is done through empowering the people through mutual image making, vision creation, mission discernment, and values clarification. Then those laity with the gift of "governings" can do the day-to-day, week-to-week, detailed administration. This avoids creating dependence and passivity and instead creates mutual care and responsibility.

We have seen how understanding leadership shapes and informs church administration. A few further comments are appropriate to pastoral clarity in the area of leadership itself. A leader is to bring perspective on the whole enterprise being led. If a man is standing in a pasture with a rope, without perspective he will not know whether he has found a rope or lost a cow.

The pastoral leader brings theological perspective to church life and mission. Without theological perspective, the community will not know whether it has found its mission or lost its identity. Being busy does not ensure being faithful; being together does not ensure being a community; being a community does not ensure being a Christian community. Theological perspective is the gift of leadership the pastor is called to exercise.

Clarity in the pastoral vocation with regard to leadership is best served by a deep appreciation for the paradoxes of leadership. I offer five paradoxes of leadership, most of which are specific articulations of the issues we have been discussing.

1. The foundation of pastoral leadership is in servanthood rather than in authority and the exercise of power and office. Hermann Hesse's story *Journey to the East* tells of a group of people on a pilgrimage. All goes well because there is a servant who attends to their needs in light of the purpose of the journey. He encourages and empowers them through song, poetry, and storytelling. One day the servant disappears, and the pilgrimage falls apart. They come to learn that their servant was actually the leader of a great priory. While the pilgrims thought he was their servant, he was their leader. He led through serving. Albert Schweitzer's comment on service is particularly applicable to pastoral leadership: "I don't know what your destiny will be, but one thing I know: the only ones among you who will be really happy are those who will have sought and found how to serve."[4]

2. The motivation for pastoral leadership is the practice of love, not the exercise of power. Being a leader is not necessarily good. The prime example of this is *Der Führer*—the leader whose leadership was based in twisted theology, self-serving mission, insatiable personal need, and the exercise of power and control.

On the other hand, Mother Teresa's leadership was based in the power of love. She reminds the pastoral leader that "We can do no great things—only small things with great love."[5]

3. The manifestation of leadership is in the articulation of image, vision, mission, and values within the community, not micromanaging the community through control and techniques. Creativity is crucial to the exercise of leadership that inspires leadership, responsibility, and the passion for life within the community. Micromanaging is death to creativity and freedom within the community. General George S. Patton, for all his faults, knew this: "If everyone is thinking alike, then somebody isn't thinking."[6] Albert Einstein encouraged people never to lose what he called a holy curiosity. Pastoral leadership that nurtures personal and communal creativity and holy curiosity serves to keep the congregation open to the future and alive to the present.

4. The cultivation of pastoral leadership begins with attention to oneself rather than attention to others. Too often a pastor develops a sense of "me against them." Why can't I get "them" to…? Why don't "they"…? The first attention of the pastor is to his or her own life. Attention to the self actually enhances attention to others. The deeper one goes into the mystery of the self, the more universally helpful or applicable one's insights become. Leadership begins with inner scrutiny, not with outer accusation. It is the willingness of the leader to be led in the ways of God, in the presence of God. It also involves the practice of self-care, the subject to which we will turn in the next chapter. Let it be noted here, however, that self-care should receive attention in times of health rather than simply being a reaction in times of illness. John F. Kennedy's admonition "The time to repair the roof is when the sun is shining"[7] is appropriate advice to pastors and congregations.

5. The real success of leadership is communal more than personal. The real test of effective pastoral leadership is not to be found in the notoriety of a single person, but in the nature of a genuine community. It is not in the accomplishments of one person, but in the accomplishments of many people. It is not in the personal aggrandizement of the leader, but in the fulfillment of many persons and their mission in community. Not all forms of leadership will build community, but effective pastoral leadership will. Vocational clarity centers the pastor in God and focuses the pastor on the people, resulting in a style of leadership that fosters community, communication, and communion in the mutuality of care. Winston Churchill knew and said this in speaking of his leadership of the

British people through their darkest hour: "It was the nation and the people dwelling all around the globe that had the lion's heart. I had the luck to be called upon to give the roar."[8]

Pastoral leadership and administration that understands and cultivates mutuality within the community could learn an important lesson from the New York Orpheus Orchestra. The point of the conductor of an orchestra is to lead, not to run all over the orchestra pit playing all the instruments. The conductor is to "orchestrate," read and understand the music, know its history and its meanings, give attention to nuances and subtleties, and enable the playing by the orchestra of a great symphony. But for that to happen, there must also be a host of trained musicians who have a passion for the music, who read and understand it, who also pay attention to nuances and subtleties, and who give voice to their instruments. The uniqueness of the New York Orpheus Orchestra is that it conducts itself. It is a "flat organization" rather than a hierarchy. This does not mean it is without leadership. Here are seven principles they follow that should inform pastors and their congregations in leadership and administrative tasks.[9]

1. People do not pay to listen to an organization, but to an orchestra.
2. No matter how hard you work, there are some things you do over and over again.
3. Identify problems together, and together look for solutions. All of us are smarter than any of us. In the beginning is chaos. So be it. Chaos always precedes the creative act.
4. Lead without telling people what to do. Leave room for their own personhood and initiative.
5. Know that the right "employees" make all the difference. In terms of right employees, develop leaders that are creative, flexible, and collegial.
6. Stand up for what you believe and encourage others to do the same. This does not mean dogmatic intractability, but the free exchange of passionate ideas.
7. Understand that God is not necessarily efficient, but passionate.

These principles, reflected on metaphorically in relationship to congregational life, its running, and its mission, can be invaluable for its creativity, communal image and esprit de corps, effectiveness, and morale.

Finally, a story by Isaac Luria from Shivhei ha-Ari focuses the issue of pastoral leadership and administration. The goal of the life of the church is often forgotten in administrative details, especially when leadership is reduced to technique. What follows is Rabbi Nancy Fuchs-Kreimer's edited version of Zalmar Schachter's recounting of this tale:

At the beginning of the sixteenth century, a man named Jacobo and his wife, Esperanza, expelled from Spain, settled in S'fat in the north of Israel. Since Jacobo knew only Spanish, he never fully understood what went on in synagogue. One Shabbat he heard the Torah verses from Leviticus 24:5–6 in which the Children of Israel are instructed to give God twelve loaves of challah in the ancient wilderness tabernacle before the Sabbath. He came home full of excitement, "Esperanza, God likes challah for Shabbat and you bake the best challah in the world. Next Friday bake twelve loaves and we can bring them to the synagogue for God."

So Esperanza baked her best challah, kneading her good intentions into the dough. Friday afternoon, when no one was around, the two brought the twelve challahs to the synagogue, arranged them neatly in the ark, said *"Buen apetito"* to God, closed the ark and left, very happy. A few minutes later the janitor came in with his broom. "Dear God," he said as he stood before the ark. "My children are starving. I need a miracle." He opened the ark and, finding the challahs inside, he smiled. He had believed that God would provide.

The next morning when the rabbi opened the ark during services, Esperanza and Jacobo saw immediately that God had eaten every loaf. They winked at each other with satisfaction. And so this continued week after week, year after year. Esperanza baked, the janitor and his family ate. Thirty years passed. One Friday, Esperanza stood before the ark and said "God, I'm sorry about the lumps in the challah. I'm getting old and my fingers don't work as well as they used to. I hope you enjoy them anyway."

At that moment, the old rabbi of the synagogue appeared and grabbed Esperanza and Jacobo by the collar. "What are you doing, you fools?" he cried.

"We are giving God his challahs."

"Don't you know that God doesn't eat?"

"You may be a rabbi, but there are some things you don't know. God most certainly does eat. In thirty years he has never left behind a crumb."

"Let's hide in the back of the synagogue and see what really happens to your challahs," said the Rabbi.

A few minutes later the janitor came in. "Dear God, I don't like to complain, but your challahs have been getting a bit lumpy lately. Still, it's keeping my family alive." He reached into the ark to get his challah and the rabbi appeared and said, "Stop, you terrible man. Maimonides has taught us that God does not have a body. He doesn't bake challah and he doesn't eat challah. All three of you have been committing the sin of anthropomorphism!"

At this, the janitor, Jacobo, and Esperanza all began to cry. The good couple was crying because they had merely wanted to serve God. The janitor was crying because he suspected this meant no more challahs. At that moment the great kabbalist Isaac Luria entered the room.

He turned to the old rabbi. "You must go home immediately and make sure your will is in order. Thirty years ago your time had come to die, but the Angel of Death was called off because God was having so much fun watching what went on in your synagogue. Now it is over, and you will be buried this week, before the Sabbath begins."

Then he turned to the weeping couple and the janitor. "Now that you know who has been eating your challahs, who has been baking your challahs, you must continue to bake them and eat them anyway. Jacobo and Esperanza must bring them every week directly to the janitor. And you must all believe with perfect faith that it is God who bakes and God who takes and that God is no less present in your lives."[10]

Concerning this tale, Rabbi Fuchs-Kreimer comments:

What was going on in the synagogue with Jacobo, Esperanza, and the janitor? They were making the world more just, and, in their innocence, they thought it had something to do with God. The good couple thought that in giving to the poor they were giving to God and the janitor thought that in receiving he was getting from God. They were all correct. The rabbi's life was extended for thirty years because during those thirty years he had, quite unintentionally, achieved the goal of the rabbinate. His synagogue was functioning the way a synagogue should.

His lay people were serving God by taking care of each other, and the Torah ark was the center of it all...A true rabbi makes the synagogue a place where people do God's work and receive God's work and thus have God in their lives.[11]

This tale mostly makes me wonder about the church and its function, the ministry and its goal. It also casts enormous light on the goal of leadership and administration in the pastoral vocation. When leadership and administration are theologically grounded rather than technique-oriented, they have at their heart the making of a congregation "where people do God's work and receive God's work and thus have God in their lives." This giving of what one has to give and this receiving of what one needs to receive becomes the meaning of Christian *koinonia*—of life together in Christ. And the whole of the life of the congregation and all its activities will be centered in worship.

CHAPTER 12

The Pastor's Survival Kit

Charles Kingsley, the Anglican cleric and novelist, used to lean from his pulpit in the parish church of Eversly in Hampshire and say earnestly to his people, "Here we are again to talk about what is really going on in your soul and mine." To this point our conversation has centered on pastoral vocational clarity. We have been talking about faithfulness in the pastoral vocation. Now we come to talk about what is going on in your soul and mine. We need to talk about faithfulness to ourselves. We need to talk about taking care of ourselves.

Everything, animate and inanimate, needs care. Without care, everything, animate and inanimate, disintegrates. Without care, houses, church buildings, cars, cities, neighborhoods fall apart. Schools, seminaries, universities, and all other institutions fall apart. Relationships fall apart. Without self-care, persons fall apart. We end this conversation where we began, recognizing that "so many people are coming and going we don't even have time to nurture ourselves." Yet self-care is an ethical mandate for pastors. Without attending to ourselves, we try to attend to others at their and our own peril.

To care is to *care about* something. It is to mind or pay attention to something or someone. It is to have a fondness for something, to love something. We have noted earlier that the word *care* comes from the Old English and old High German word for "lament." Care is, therefore, painstaking and watchful attention that results in the necessary expenditure of time, energy, and materials to keep something in good working order. Self-care is literally to have a

133

fondness for ourselves, to love ourselves, to pay attention to ourselves and our own needs. Too often a pastor's expenditure of self-giving exceeds the pastor's deposits of self-care, resulting in emotional or physical bankruptcy.

The reasons to give attention to self-care are self-evident. No one else will take care of you. It is the responsibility of adulthood and maturity to care for ourselves and to set up systems, structures, and relationships that can assist us in paying attention to ourselves. In other words, self-care goes beyond being our own physician, therapist, and spiritual director. Pastors need others in order to be and become themselves. Pastors need a "thou" to remain an "I." We are persons in and through those who call us into being. Self-care is also important because it is out of the center of who we are that we minister. Without attention to the center, when we reach for the irreducible and nonnegotiable "I," we will find a void. Self-care as an ethical mandate relates to the foundation of ethical action in relationship to others. The Hippocratic oath of "do no harm" is applicable to pastoral work. Without attention to ourselves, we can become a danger to others. Systematic loving attention to our own needs, fears, desires, wounds, hopes, ego, hungers, and drives is critical if we are to live among the people with availability and in vulnerability, the only way we can actually minister with integrity.

Failure in self-care among pastors has devastating results. The consequences for pastors in varying degrees of complexity can be melancholy, depression, breakdown, stress and stress-related illnesses, addictions, inability to stay in the pastorate for the long-distance run, weariness (not just tiredness, but the kind of weariness that results in ennui, the "boredom unto death"), and loss of faith. The consequences for others (family, friends, congregations) in varying degrees of complexity can be broken relationships, violated boundaries, abuse, disintegration of continuity, and ruptured communities. The catchall term for these maladies of the spirit and disorders of the psyche is *burnout*.

It is not an uncommon disease or dis-ease among pastors who fail to come to terms with their own limitations and who do not look after themselves. Burnout—literally, burning until the fire burns itself out—is severe physical, mental, and spiritual exhaustion. It is usually accompanied by loss of control, loss of challenge or interest, and loss of commitment or faith. Burnout is much easier to prevent than it is to treat.

Why, then, do so many pastors neglect the care and cure of their own souls? Recognizing that many causes, situations, contexts, and circumstances can contribute to burnout and that there are no easy answers or quick fixes, there are still a few fundamental issues that a pastor with vocational clarity can address.

The first is to engage ministry with a spirit of Christian realism rather than pious romanticism. One of C. G. Jung's criticisms of Christian theology is that it didn't take evil seriously enough. This is particularly true of pastors who enter ministry with a romantic view of the pastoral vocation—helping people, serving God, saving the world, believing people will do better if they only know better, bringing peace and blessed assurance. This is usually accompanied by a rather romantic view of Jesus—meek and mild, sweet and gentle, kind and considerate. It is forgotten that Jesus came to make forgiveness of sin possible, not to make it unnecessary because people are basically good. It is forgotten that the spiritual life is lived in confrontation with the principalities and powers, against the world rulers of this present darkness, against the spiritual hosts of wickedness. Entering into ministry and maturing in ministry will involve a spirit of Christian realism in which evil is taken seriously, decadence is recognized, and the terrain of the world, the flesh, and the devil (to use the words of *The Book of Common Prayer*) is not a quaint fairyland, but the realm of pastoral engagement. This realm of engagement is not just "out there" but "in here," within the soul of the pastor. Christian realism will not allow us to forget that there is a cup to drink and a baptism with which to be baptized. It will not let us forget that there is a cross at the center of the Christian story. And it will not allow us to forget that we are servants, not saviors. Pious romanticism, on the other hand, is fed by overblown and intemperate language resulting in unrealistic expectations and false optimism. During my college days I attended and participated in an organization called "Mission Study." The slogan of this group was: "We can take the world for Christ in our generation!" Christian realism began to develop in my consciousness when, early on in ministry, I realized I could not take a single block of my own street for Christ. Christian realism also helped me to recognize that it would be a lifelong struggle for my own heart to be taken for Christ—that an understanding of needing Christ as savior belongs more to the end of the road of Christian discipleship than to the beginning. It becomes for many of us an existential truth only when we have tried to walk the way of discipleship. This kind of Christian realism can begin the process of recognizing the need for self-care among clergy.

Another reason pastors do not practice adequate self-care, not unrelated to pious romanticism, is the feeling that if we are doing the work of God, God will take care of us. It is the sense that any problems, doubts, difficulties, uncertainties, or moral failures are signs of spiritual weakness and a lack of faith. It also stems from the delusion that "wearing out" in the ministry is a sign of devotion and commitment, of heroic deeds of the faithful Christian soldier.

We sometimes fail to attend to our own needs because our basic need is the *need to be needed*. It is a matter of self-justification. Helping others makes us feel good about ourselves. We sometimes feel that attending to ourselves is a demonstration of selfishness.

Fear is another contributing factor to the lack of self-care among clergy. We have the irrational fear that if we are not able to satisfy all of the people all of the time, we will be failures. Or we have the irrational fear that the congregation will not survive without us. And under this is the deeper fear that perhaps they will learn that they *can* survive without us!

In addition to *reasons* for lack of attention among clergy to self-care, there are what I consider *excuses*: I don't have the time; I am too busy; I am too successful; opportunities of self-care are not available or provided by my denomination; or I'm doing just fine, thank you very much. Most of the *excuses* for not practicing self-care are self-serving in nature. But most of the *reasons* for not practicing self-care are theological in nature. They stem from incomplete or inadequate understandings of human nature, of the nature and complexity of evil, and of the nature of God, Jesus, the Holy Spirit, and the processes of saving grace. They are rooted in pious romanticism rather than Christian realism, in fantasy more than in hope. Like everything else we have been saying about vocational clarity in the pastorate, self-care is to be approached not by searching for techniques and gimmicks, but through theology. The pastor's survival kit will include a theology of ministry, a theology of self-care, and a theology of spirituality.

A Theology of Ministry

The subject of our conversation together has been about a theology of ministry. Any theology of ministry is rooted in vocational clarity and Christian realism. It is vital for every pastor to develop his or her own theology of ministry, not in abstractions or general goals, but in specificity and particularity. Equally vital, though often neglected, is the sharing of that theology of ministry with the specific congregation or parish that one serves. It is impossible for a theological community to function sympathetically and supportively with its pastor if a theology of ministry for both the pastor and the congregation is not developed and articulated. This is also true for the development and articulation of a theology of self-care and a theology of spirituality. As these theologies of ministry, self-care, and spirituality change, alter, or develop to meet changing needs, differing contexts, and new challenges, the theologies need to be revised and articulated within the community. The shared praxis–based educational method so clearly propounded by Thomas Groome[1] is a helpful model for the articulation and practical application of the theology of ministry, the theology of self-care, and the theology of spirituality that form the foundation of healthy relationships between the pastor and the people. Groome defines praxis from the Greek as "purposeful, intentional, and reflectively chosen ethical action."[2] In a theology of ministry, praxis is purposeful, intentional, and reflectively chosen understanding and practice of the pastoral ministry. The "shared" aspect of a theology of ministry has to do with the pastor's relationship with the congregation, including conversations regarding pastoral clarity. Just as no one becomes a Christian by oneself, no one becomes a pastor by oneself. Pastoring takes place in a communal context. Therefore, pastoral vocational clarity and a theology of ministry are shaped by interaction within the community where the pastoral functions occur.

Five movements in Groome's shared praxis approach to Christian religious education are informative for the development of a theology of ministry between a pastor and a congregation. The five movements are (1) naming present action, (2) critical reflection on that action, (3) dialogue, (4) attention to the story of the tradition, and (5) vision-making toward a new action. The naming of the action in developing a theology of ministry is a mutual conversation between the pastor and the people regarding how the ministry has been practiced in this particular context, what the various expectations are of the pastor, and what the pastor's own understandings of the pastoral vocation are. Critical reflection involves analysis of what has been named, including areas of coherence and areas of conflict or collision. Dialogue offers the opportunity for pastor and people alike to share their views and emotional reactions to the analysis that has revealed the areas of conflict and cohesion, especially regarding things in present action that are not working or cannot work, things that are unhealthy for both pastor and parish. Attention to the story of the tradition begins to lift up and make available the ways in which the church has dealt with issues of pastoral clarity and ecclesial identity and mission, including both the ancient past and the more recent history of the congregation. This attention to the story enables the community to know its history. It can then deal with that story in both conserving and transmitting ways as well as in liberative and transformative ways. Out of the previous four movements, the congregation and pastor can begin to develop a mutual vision for their future ministry together.

In light of Groome's five movements, the following questions are helpful in developing one's own theology of ministry in tandem with the congregation's needs and understandings.

- What is your image of a pastor?
- What is your image of the ministry?
- What is your image of the parish or congregation you serve?
- What do you like to do in ministry?
- What do you not like to do in ministry?
- What are you good at? What are your gifts? What are your strengths?
- What are you not so good at? What are your limitations? What are your weaknesses?
- What is your worldly context?
- How do you measure success?

The point of these questions is to begin to get to really know yourself in relationship to the pastoral vocation. Recognizing and articulating limitations as well as strengths, dislikes as well as likes, is important. No pastor has universal expertise. It is a powerful move within a congregation for the pastor to be able to say, "I'm really not very good at that. Let's talk about it." Only in this way can one begin to minister out of the center of one's own being. Only when one ministers out of the center of one's being can there be the stamina and the energy for long-term ministry that does not end in burnout and bitterness. Otherwise, the pastor's personhood and vocational identity are not coherent. There is a fracture in the ontological foundation. The pastor's vitality is eroded, and the pastor ends up as a resentful functionary of everyone else's projections and expectations.

Attempting, consciously or unconsciously, to be the functionary of everyone else's expectations leads to what Donald Smith once called the syndrome of "clergy in the crossfire."[3] Enormous amounts of grief and heartbreak can be avoided for both the pastor and the congregation if both address together this issue early in the pastorate and consistently in the course of the ministry, using the shared praxis approach. An assorted variety of claims can be made on a pastor, and he or she can be pulled in many different directions. Constituency claims within a single congregation can include those from boards, elders, deacons, women's fellowship, men's fellowship, youth fellowship, Sunday schools, committees, choirs, veteran members, new members, nonmembers, singles, families, nontraditional families, and various special cause or interest groups. Functional claims within a single congregation can include preacher, teacher, counselor, visitor, evangelist, prophet, social activist, administrator, public relations person, social events director, editor, and fund raiser. Persona claims within a single congregation can include dynamic leader, spiritual friend, scholarly student, holy saint, radical prophet, moral pillar, and *bon vivant*. Personal claims within a single congregation can include those from a spouse, a child, a friend, or a colleague. There are so many role claims made on a pastor in these different ways that it is no wonder the pastor feels torn in so many directions. Some of the role claims are ambiguous. Some are confused. Some are incompatible. Some are in conflict. Some are impossible. It is certainly impossible to fulfill all expectations and meet all projections. Without a center based in a theology of ministry and deep running knowledge of the self, a pastor is almost certainly doomed to a sense of failure to meet expectations. The sense of failure often turns into disillusionment and burnout.

Dietrich Bonhoeffer's 1945 poem "Who Am I" poignantly illustrates a pastor's dilemma, even if the dilemma falls under less dramatic and frightening circumstances than Bonhoeffer's.

Who am I? They often tell me
I stepped from my cell's confinement
Calmly, cheerfully, firmly,
Like a squire from his country-house.
Who am I? They often tell me
I used to speak to my warders
Freely and friendly and clearly,
As though it were mine to command.

Who am I? They also tell me
I bore the days of misfortune
Equably, smilingly, proudly,
Like one accustomed to win.
Am I then really all that which other men tell of?
Or am I only what I myself know of myself?
Restless and longing and sick, like a bird in a cage,
Struggling for breath, as though hands were compressing
    my throat,
Yearning for colors, for flowers, for the voices of birds,
Thirsting for words of kindness, for neighborliness,
Tossing in expectation of great events,
Powerlessly trembling for friends at an infinite distance,
Weary and empty of praying, at thinking, at making,
Faint, and ready to say farewell to it all.
Who am I? This or the other?
Am I one person today and tomorrow another?
Am I both at once? A hypocrite before others,
And before myself a contemptibly woebegone weakling?
Or is something within me still like a beaten army,
Fleeing in disorder from victory already achieved?
Who am I? They mock me, these lonely questions of mine.
Whoever I am, Thou knowest, O God, I am Thine! [4]

The confusion, internal conflict, uncertainty, and doubt expressed by Bonhoeffer has been felt in varying degrees by most pastors. The struggle for clarity and coherence is at the heart of faithfulness and will last a lifetime. The final lines of this poem are a witness to Bonhoeffer's vocational clarity in the midst of human suffering, personal grief, and contextual confusion.

Living and working out of a theology of ministry is essential to a pastor's survival kit. It is one of the ways the pastor can catch a breath—that is, be inspired. Theological "breath catching," or inspiration, can be received through three types of breathing: Breathe deeply from the past; breathe regularly from the present; and breathe consistently the "kind of air" you like, the air that refreshes you—that is, mountain air, desert air, garden air, and the like. What do I mean by these fairly strange metaphors?

I find inspiration in the ministry by breathing the air of the tradition. By this I simply mean staying close to the classics of theology that have given life and breath to the history of the church and the pastoral vocation. It means breathing the air that has been the product of previous inspirations. I believe it is good to graze among the books in one's library, inhaling here from Hildegard of Bingen and there from Gregory of Nyssa and then from Martin Luther and again from Walter Rauschenbusch or Evelyn Underhill. In other words, there is a freshness and invigoration that comes from dipping in and out of a wide variety of theological resources that provide inspiration when one is doing work within the sometimes stifling climate of mundane day-to-day pastoral routine.

I also find inspiration by breathing the air of the present. By this I simply mean staying current in theological, historical, and biblical studies. It is very difficult for a pastor to be a professional scholar in the true sense of the word *scholar.* That is a vocation in and of itself. But a pastor can be scholarly and theological. The pastor can breathe the air of theological and historical scholarship and find inspiration renewed and imagination invigorated. Breathing this air of contemporary scholarship through books, articles, journals, and conversations can revitalize and refresh pastoral work.

Breathing the kind of air one likes is also important for catching one's breath. There are times when a walk through an aspen grove on an early autumn morning near my home can refresh my spirit like nothing else. I like it. I feel at home there. For others it happens in the soft air of a desert twilight. For others it is found in the fragrance of a garden. The point I am trying to make is that there is "air" we really like, air we find energizing and restorative to the spirit. I believe pastors can find inspiration by developing one specific area of theological study that they like and then breathing that air deeply. It is to find one's focus in a particular subject and then to make that subject the air one breaths, the field of one's lifetime of study. This can be a biblical book, a theological theme, a particular doctrine, a particular person—whatever. But whatever it is, it gives a lens through which to look at all other areas of study. By going deeply into one area, by breathing deeply in one subject, one gains perspective on all other areas of theology and pastoral work. It contributes to pastoral inspiration.

A Theology of Self-care

Ministry is more than a living, but it is less than a life. Once again, a theology of self-care is rooted in pastoral vocational clarity. That clarity is the foundation for avoiding confusing who you are with what you do, or how busy you are as validation of your worth. The rhythms of creation and rest, work and play, community and solitude, expenditure and renewal are built into our humanity. Attention to Sabbath rest is as important as attention to faithful work. A theology of self-care is greatly enhanced by a deep-seated understanding of and appreciation for the doctrine of the Sabbath.

If care is "painstaking and watchful attention," then what is it the pastor is to attend to in the care of self? Attending to the body and its physical and psychic needs is a beginning point. This involves proper diet and proper exercise. It involves adequate rest. Nothing looks good when one is exhausted. It includes attention to sexual and emotional needs as well as play and recreation and hobbies. It will incorporate nurturing provided by the arts, drama, music, and literature. It will entail getting interested and staying interested in activities outside the church and unrelated to ministry. Attending to the body's physical and psychic needs also requires an honesty about one's coping mechanisms—do they involve the use of too much alcohol, the abuse of drugs, emotional withdrawal, misdirected and/or inappropriate anger? Awareness of depression, including attention to its manifestations and treatment of its causes, is critical, as depression can be connected to the functions and misfunctions of body chemistry.

Attending to family relationships is part of self-care. This attention should be carried out in private and with sensitivity. In most cases, the pastor is the one who has responded to a call, and the spouse and children should not be expected to live in lockstep with that call. The pastor's family members should be granted the freedom of their own personal identities and faith journeys. They are not an extension of the pastoral persona. Nonetheless, much grief has filled family relationships through the pastor's insistence that spouse or children be a reflection of his or her "godly presence" and an augmentation of his or her ministry. Years of experience in dealing with my own family issues, and those that have been part of the conversations at A Mountain Retreat with other pastors and their spouses or children, have convinced me that it is very difficult for a pastor's spouse and a pastor's children to keep faith alive. Attention to family issues begins with the pastor's being clear with the congregation about these matters—and clear with his or her own family. This includes the recognition that spouses and children of pastors need other pastors than the family member—here the pastor is to be husband or wife, father or mother.

Attending to security needs also contributes to self-care. Financial worries can erode the spirit. Short- and long-term budget planning, living within one's means, and requesting adequate financial compensation are not acts of selfishness but of self-care. Inappropriate spending and compulsive purchasing are often signs of depression or deep emotional conflict.

Attending to the development of appropriate support systems inside and outside the church is also a nonnegotiable factor in self-care. Maya Angelou reflects this need beautifully.

> Lying, thinking
> Last night
> How to find my soul a home
> Where water is not thirsty
> And bread loaf is not stone
> I came up with one thing
> And I don't believe I'm wrong
> That nobody
> But nobody
> Can make it out here alone. [5]

One simply cannot "make it all alone" in ministry. Having people around all the time is not the same as developing intentional support systems. Support systems should be developed to care for technical, professional, spiritual, and emotional needs. Developing a group of "technical" advisors in various areas such as administration, pastoral counseling, and theological reflection is of enormous help. It contributes to self-care by eliminating the need to be an expert in all areas and can free the pastor from a constant sense of inadequacy. The meeting of professional needs can be developed through recognizing that one is part of "a holy ministry" and not an independent spiritual entrepreneur. Collegial groups for study and theological reflection can contribute to professional support. Within the congregation, a well-trained and active pastor/parish council can help with problems, affirmations, feedback, accountability, and reality testing. Support for one's spiritual needs includes developing a consistent relationship with a confessor or spiritual director. Finally, developing a significant supportive friend or group of friends is indispensable to self-care.

One of the most important factors contributing to the long-distance run in ministry, for avoiding burnout and the hazards to virtue inherent in the pastoral vocation, is for ministers to develop camaraderie with a few colleagues who will keep the demons of isolation, loneliness, competitiveness, self-righteousness, and humorlessness at bay. Otherwise, pastors are subject to a "me against the world" mentality, which results in a pinched and narrow spirit, an over-sensitive ego, an unattractive self-righteousness, and a life devoid of humble joy and courageous celebration. Let me try to say as clearly as possible what these friendships have meant to my life in ministry. Without these companions in the way, without their friendship, I would be a poorer believer than I am or perhaps no believer at all. For it is in them and with them that I have caught the sometimes elusive glimpse of Christ in the world. My friends have helped me believe, and at times have believed for me, when I could not believe for myself. This has been true in good times as well as in times of the darkest depression.

Their holy laughter has helped to debunk the principalities and powers of this age and to desacralize the claims of our contemporary idols (including that closest and most persistent of all idols, the idol of oneself, the Narcissus within me). Laughter has helped us all to dance irreverently before the false gods of power and popularity and pride. In short, their gift of humor in the fellowship of laughter has lightened many a load, lifted many a discouragement, and defused the debilitating overseriousness with which one tends to take both oneself and the pronouncements of ecclesiastical or governmental political powers.

Furthermore, the counsel of these few close friends has been influential in protecting against the inclination in me toward individualism and the insidious temptation toward the cult of personality that is so prevalent in ministry.

Finally, they have been my confessors, granting in the name of Christ the absolution of my sins. In this capacity they have been uncomfortably rigorous. They have been corrective without being judgmental. They have offered challenge without competitiveness. And they have never let me go. To have such friends in the ministry is a gift of grace beyond words and an essential ingredient in the pastor's survival kit.

In addition to attending to physical and psychic health issues, family concerns, security needs, and support systems, self-care will also involve maintenance structures. I begin here with the simple reminder to take days off from pastoral work regularly. Ministry is a marathon, not a sprint. Sunday is a workday for the pastor. The pastor should have a "weekend," meaning two days a week, not including a Sunday, for attention to the personal life. One of these days would be the day for regular family chores, errand running, and family time. The other day should be for the pastor's own re-creation. Other maintenance structures along this line include time for vacation and continuing education, as well as time for retreats, conventions, and professional meetings.

Because the experience of God is at the heart of pastoral vocational clarity, regular spiritual retreats should be a part of a pastor's maintenance structures. This brings us to the last theological dimension of a pastor's survival kit to be discussed.

A Theology of Spirituality

Spiritual formation has been at the heart of these conversations about pastoral vocational clarity. We have recognized that many pastors live as slaves to time as if Christ had never "tamed" time, as if time or the lack thereof were the enemy. Rhythms of grace, silences of solitude, patterns of prayer, and the patience of meditation often are absent from the pastor's survival kit. Some have said that the only things to disappear faster than study from the pastor's life after leaving the seminary and entering the parish are the spiritual disciplines. Perhaps it is because so little time, attention, and intention are given to spiritual formation in the first place. So walking in faith becomes running in works. Resting in God becomes questing for relevance. Waiting in hope becomes striving in anxiety.

One of the most important functions that comes from pastoral vocational clarity and feeds back into it is the practice of the spiritual life. Some pastors find it helpful to set aside a day a week for prayer, a day a month for spiritual retreat, and a week a year for personal or communal/collegial spiritual retreat and renewal. Such a practice will not come easily, for both secular and church cultures mitigate against it. But without developing and practicing a theology of spirituality, all our preachments, gimmicks, techniques, pieties, and professionalisms are a vanity and a striving after wind.

Desert hearts indeed. But still a place not only of danger but of opportunity. "Lord, teach us to pray." In the asking, the seeking, and the knocking, may the way be opened beneath our feet to the living fountains of God's sustaining grace.

CHAPTER 13

How Beautiful Are the Feet

Some of these thoughts were shared with me by my friend and colleague, Rev. Phillip Johnson (see footnote 2 in chapter 3), in a discussion we held on the nature and content of ordination sermons. They are based on Isaiah 40:6–11 and Romans 10:13–17.

From the ear to the heart to the mouth—and then to another's ear. This is how the gospel makes its way. From hearing to believing to confessing to hearing. If our salvation were a system of knowledge, we could know God by the insight of the mind. If our salvation were founded on morals, we could come to God by the power of our moral will. If our salvation were a this-worldly achievement, we could know it by our seeing. But because our salvation comes from beyond our seeing and knowing and willing, we must know God by hearsay. We must come to know God only by hearing a word that comes from afar. The saving truth of God travels through history and around the world and around the parish, not as a theory to be comprehended or a moral program to be enacted or a puzzle to be solved, but as tidings to be believed.

But how are they to hear without someone to proclaim him? And how are they to proclaim him unless they are sent? As it is written, "How beautiful are the feet [literally, the arrival] of those who bring good news!" (Rom. 10:15, paraphrasing Isa. 52:7).

How beautiful is the vocation, the pastoral office, to which one is called. How beautiful the intelligence soaked (baptized) by daily discipline in the words and images of Holy Scripture, so that it may hear and speak the mysteries of God's saving work. How beautiful the mind transformed by scripture into a genuinely pastoral and theological intelligence for the sake of the community. *Not that the intelligence claims any beauty of its own. For the human intelligence will wither and fade, but the Word of our God will stand forever.*

How beautiful the passionate heart bent every day toward the needs of the people who are famished for the word of God. Not only the faithful who gather but the wandering ones who have no pastor, no hymns to sing, no real community where they belong, and who have not heard the story of their Savior. *Not that the preacher's passion has any integrity of its own. Our passion and compassion daily will wither and fade, but the Word of our God burns hot forever.*

How beautiful is the ministry that really trusts and reposes in the Lord's means of grace—the word and the sacraments—and that does not worry overmuch about gimmicks, techniques, methods, public relations, or programs. *For the gimmicks quickly wither and fade and tomorrow are thrown into the fire, but the Word of our God stands forever.*

How beautiful is the personal and moral struggle suffered for the sake of this call. The struggle to despise all charismatic appeal except the true charisma of the gospel; the struggle to embrace obscurity and the hidden disciplines and to be faithful when no one is watching or evaluating; the struggle to be pure in heart and body; the struggle to be an example to others, to be faithful in a liberated obedience to God's law; the struggle to allow something of the beauty of the call to penetrate one's whole being. *Not that the power of this ministry rests in our own moral integrity, which withers and fades under the perfect judgment of God's Word, which stands forever.*

How beautiful the pastoral journey from Lord's Day to Lord's Day. How beautiful the feet that really stick to the path leading back and forth from prayer, study, catechism, pastoral visitation, preaching, baptizing, and celebrating the eucharist, which, of course, turns out to be at least a full-time job and doesn't really require a lot of extras to keep one busy or to make one feel legitimate. *For our feeling good and self-legitimization will wither and fade, but the Word of our God stands forever.*

How beautiful the feet. How focused the heart. How concentrated the mind. How disciplined the habits. How unmistakable the frameworks. How ordered the time. How passionate the spirit. How redemptive the suffering. How centered the life. How joyful the ministry. How important clarity in the pastoral vocation.

A Bibliography for Pastors

It is assumed that the theological pastor will maintain an updated bibliography in the various disciplines that are a part of the pastoral vocation: for example, biblical studies, systematic theology, pastoral theology, church history, ecclesiology, homiletics, ethics, sociology of religion, and so forth. The purpose of this *pastoral bibliography* is to focus on three areas: (1) the pastoral vocation, because here we are concerned with the person in the practice of ministry in its wholeness; (2) the pastoral devotion, because the pastor should never be far away from prayer and the spiritual disciplines; and (3) the pastor and literature, because the pastor should never be far away from great literature and the use of language.

The Pastoral Vocation

Anderson, Ray S., ed. *Theological Foundations for Ministry.* Edinburgh: T & T Clark, 1979.

Bass, Dorothy, ed. *Practicing Our Faith: A Way of Life for Searching People.* San Francisco: Jossey-Bass, 1997.

Bloede, Louis W. *The Effective Pastor.* Minneapolis: Fortress Press, 1996.

Bonhoeffer, Dietrich. *The Cost of Discipleship.* Translated by R. H. Fuller. New York: Macmillan, 1949.

———. *Letters and Papers from Prison.* Translated by R. H. Fuller. Edited by Eberhard Bethge. London: SCM Press, 1953.

———. *Life Together.* Translated with an Introduction by John W. Doberstein. New York: Harper and Row, 1954.

———. *Spiritual Care.* Translated by Jay C. Rochelle. Philadelphia: Fortress Press, 1985.

Bratcher, Edward B. *The Walk-on-Water Syndrome.* With a Foreword by Wayne Oates. Waco, Tx.: Word Books, 1984.

Buechner, Frederick. *Telling the Truth: The Gospel as Tragedy, Comedy and Fairy Tale.* San Francisco: Harper and Row, 1977.

Buttrick, David. *Homiletic.* Philadelphia: Fortress Press, 1987.

Campbell, Alastair V. *Rediscovering Pastoral Care*. London: Darton, Longman and Todd, 1981.

Clebsch, William A., and Charles Jaekle. *Pastoral Care in Historical Perspective*. New York: Jason Aronson, 1983.

Craddock, Fred B. *Preaching*. Nashville: Abingdon Press, 1985.

Dawn, Marva, and Eugene Peterson. *The Unnecessary Pastor*. Grand Rapids, Mich.: Eerdmans. Vancouver: Regent College Publishing, 2000.

Farmer, H. H. *The Servant of the Word*. Philadelphia: Fortress Press, 1942.

Fisher, David. *The 21st Century Pastor*. Grand Rapids, Mich.: Zondervan, 1996.

Fuchs-Kreimer, Nancy. "Holiness, Justice and the Rabbinate." *CrossCurrents: The Journal of the Association for Religion and Intellectual Life* 42 (Summer 1992): 212–27.

Hall, Douglas John. *Why Christian? For Those On the Edge of Faith*. Minneapolis: Fortress Press, 1998.

Holmes, Urban T. III. *Ministry and Imagination*. New York: Seabury Press, 1981.

Hunter, Victor L., and Phillip Johnson. *The Human Church in the Presence of Christ*. Macon, Ga.: Mercer University Press, 1985.

Knox, John. *The Integrity of Preaching*. Nashville: Abingdon Press, 1957.

Luther, Martin. *Luther's Works*. Vol. 41. Philadelphia: Fortress Press, 1963.

Marney, Carlyle. *Priests to Each Other*. Valley Forge, Pa.: Judson Press, 1974.

McBurney, Louis. *Every Pastor Needs a Pastor*. Carbondale, Colo.: Pastoral Ministry Resources, 1977.

Messer, Donald E. *Contemporary Images of Christian Ministry*. Nashville: Abingdon Press, 1989.

Migliore, Daniel L. *The Power of God*. Philadelphia: Westminster Press, 1983.

Niebuhr, Reinhold. *Leaves from the Notebook of a Tamed Cynic*. New York: Meridian Books, 1929, 1957.

Nouwen, Henri J. M. *Creative Ministry*. Garden City: Doubleday, 1978.

———. *In the Name of Jesus*. New York: Crossroad, 2000.

———. *The Living Reminder*. Minneapolis: Seabury Press, 1977.

———. *The Way of the Heart*. San Francisco: Harper, 1981.

Osborn, Ronald E. *In Christ's Place*. St. Louis: Bethany Press, 1967.

Oswald, Roy M. *Cross the Boundary: Between Seminary and Parish.* Bethesda: The Alban Institute. (Published on demand from Special Papers and Research Reports.)

Palmer, Parker J. *Let Your Life Speak: Listening to the Voice of Vocation.* San Francisco: Jossey-Bass, 2000.

Peterson, Eugene H. *The Contemplative Pastor.* Grand Rapids, Mich.: Eerdmans, 1989.

———. *Five Smooth Stones for Pastoral Work.* Atlanta: John Knox Press, 1980.

———. *Under the Unpredictable Plant.* Grand Rapids, Mich.: Eerdmans, 1992.

———. *Working the Angles.* Grand Rapids, Mich.: Eerdmans, 1987.

Proctor, Samuel D., and Gardner C. Taylor. *We Have This Ministry: The Heart of the Pastor's Vocation.* Valley Forge, Pa.: Judson Press, 1996.

Scherer, Paul. *For We Have This Treasure.* New York: Harper and Brothers, 1944.

Shawchuck, Norman, and Roger Heuser. *Leading the Congregation.* Nashville: Abingdon Press, 1993.

Sims, Bennett J. *Servanthood: Leadership for the Third Millennium.* Boston: Cowley Publications, 1997.

Sittler, Joseph. *The Ecology of Faith.* Philadelphia: Muhlenberg Press, 1961.

Smith, Donald P. *Clergy in the Crossfire.* Philadelphia: Westminster Press, 1973.

———. *Empowering Ministry: Ways to Grow in Effectiveness.* Louisville: Westminster John Knox Press, 1996.

SteinhoffSmith, Roy Herndon. *The Mutuality of Care.* St. Louis: Chalice Press, 1999.

Stortz, Martha Ellen. *Pastor Power.* Nashville: Abingdon Press, 1993.

Underhill, Evelyn. "God Is the Interesting Thing." *The Christian Century,* 31 October 1990, 998.

Walker, Daniel D. *The Human Problems of the Minister.* New York: Harper and Brothers, 1960.

Weems, Lovett H. *Church Leadership.* Foreword by Rosabeth Moss Kanter. Nashville: Abingdon Press, 1993.

Weil, Simone. *Gravity and Grace.* New York: Putnam, 1952.

———. *Waiting for God.* Translated by Emma Gruafurd. With an Introduction by Leslie A. Fiedler. New York: Putnam, 1951.

Williams, Daniel Day. *The Minister and the Care of Souls.* New York: Harper, 1961.

The Pastoral Devotion

Bloom, Anthony. *Beginning to Pray.* New York: Paulist Press, 1970.

Book of Common Prayer. Minneapolis: Seabury Press, 1979.

Chesterton, G. K. *The Everlasting Man.* New York: Dodd, Mead and Company, 1925.

Foster, Richard J. *Celebration of Discipline.* San Francisco: Harper and Row, 1978.

Foster, Richard J., and James Bryan Smith. *Devotional Classics.* San Francisco: Harper and Row, 1993.

Gomes, Peter J. *The Good Book: Reading the Bible with Mind and Heart.* New York: William Morrow and Company, 1996.

Ignatius, St. *The Spiritual Exercises of St. Ignatius.* Translated by Anthony Mottola. With an Introduction by Robert W. Gleason. New York: Doubleday, 1989.

Job, Rueben P., and Norman Shawchuck. *A Guide to Prayer for Ministers and Other Servants.* Nashville: Upper Room, 1983.

Kurtz, Ernest, and Katherine Ketcham. *A Spirituality of Imperfection: Storytelling and the Journey to Wholeness.* New York: Bantam Books, 1994.

Nouwen, Henri J. M. *Lifesigns: Intimacy, Fecundity, and Ecstasy in Christian Perspective.* New York: Doubleday, 1989.

———. *Reaching Out: The Three Movements of the Spiritual Life.* New York: Doubleday, 1975.

Parachin, Janet W. *Engaged Spirituality: Ten Lives of Contemplation and Action.* St. Louis: Chalice Press, 1999.

Tugwell, Simon. *Prayer: Living with God.* 2 vols. Dublin: Veritas Publications, 1974.

Underhill, Evelyn. *The Life of the Spirit and the Life of Today.* San Francisco: Harper and Row, 1922, 1986.

———. *The Spiritual Life.* London: Hodder and Stoughton, 1937, 1938, 1955.

The Pastor and Literature (Selections)

Albom, Mitch. *Tuesdays with Morrie: An Old Man, A Young Man, and Life's Greatest Lesson.* New York: Doubleday, 1997.

Bernanos, Georges. *The Diary of a Country Priest.* Translated by Pamela Morris. New York: Macmillan, 1937.

Buechner, Frederick. *Godric.* San Francisco: Harper and Row, 1980.

———. *Lion Country.* San Francisco: Harper and Row, 1971.

———. *Love Feast.* San Francisco: Harper and Row, 1974.

———. *Open Heart.* San Francisco: Harper and Row, 1972.

————. *Treasure Hunt.* San Francisco: Harper and Row, 1977.

Conroy, Pat. *The Great Santini.* New York: Bantam, 1987.

————. *The Prince of Tides.* New York: Bantam, 1987.

De Vries, Peter. *The Blood of the Lamb.* Boston: Little, Brown and Company, 1961.

Eliot, T. S. *The Complete Poems and Plays.* New York: Harcourt, Brace and World, 1952.

Gardner, Martin. *The Flight of Peter Fromm.* Los Altos, Calif.: William Kaufmann, 1973.

Greene, Graham. *Brighton Rock.* New York: Viking Press, 1956.

————. *Monsignor Quixote.* London: Bodley Head, 1982.

————. *The Power and the Glory.* New York: Bantam, 1954.

Hawkins, Peter S. *The Language of Grace.* Cambridge: Cowley Publications, 1983.

Irving, John. *A Prayer for Owen Meany.* New York: Morrow, 1989.

————. *The World According to Garp.* New York: Ballantine, 1990.

Morrison, Toni. *Beloved.* New York: Alfred A. Knopf, 1987.

Muggeridge, Malcolm. *Chronicles of Wasted Time.* Washington, D.C.: Regnery Gateway, 1972.

————. *Jesus Rediscovered.* London: Collins, 1969.

————. *A Third Testament.* Boston: Little, Brown and Company, 1976.

Murdoch, Iris. *Acastos: Two Platonic Dialogues.* New York: Viking Penguin, 1988.

————. *The Bell.* New York: Viking Penguin, 1987.

————. *The Nice and the Good.* New York: Viking Penguin, 1978.

————. *Nuns and Soldiers.* New York: Viking Penguin, 1982.

————. *The Sacred and Profane Love Machine.* New York: Viking Penguin, 1984.

————. *The Sea, the Sea.* New York: Viking Penguin, 1980.

O'Connor, Flannery. *The Complete Stories.* New York: Farrar, Strauss and Giroux, 1971.

————. *The Habit of Being.* Edited with an Introduction by Sally Fitzgerald. New York: Vintage Books, 1979.

Percy, Walker. *Lost in the Cosmos: The Last Self-Help Book.* New York: Farrar, Strauss and Giroux, 1983.

————. *Love in the Ruins.* New York: Farrar, Strauss and Giroux, 1971.

————. *The Second Coming.* New York: Ivy Books, 1990.

————. *The Thanatos Syndrome.* New York: Farrar, Strauss and Giroux, 1987.

Powers, J. F. *Wheat That Springeth Green.* New York: Alfred A. Knopf, 1988.

Saint-Exupéry, Antoine de. *The Little Prince.* Translated by Katherine
    Woods. New York: Harcourt, Brace, and World, 1943.
Stegner, Wallace. *Crossing to Safety.* New York: Random House, 1987.
Updike, John. *In the Beauty of the Lilies.* New York: Alfred A. Knopf,
    1996.
———. *A Month of Sundays.* New York: Alfred A. Knopf, 1975.
———. *Roger's Version.* New York: Alfred A. Knopf, 1986.
Wiesel, Elie. *The Gates of the Forest.* New York: Harper, 1966.
———. *Night.* New York: Bantam, 1982.

Notes

Chapter 1: Confusions and Current Conditions

[1]Mark 6:7–13, 30–31.

[2]Joseph Sittler, *The Ecology of Faith* (Philadelphia: Muhlenberg Press, 1959).

[3]Jackson W. Carroll, *Ministry as Reflective Practice: A New Look at the Professional Model* (Washington, D.C.: Alban Institute, 1986), 30.

[4]Consider Exodus 17, 19—25, 32—34; the Elijah cycle of stories; the ministry of John the Baptist; the temptation of Jesus; Paul's stay in Arabia.

[5]In Donald E. Messer, *Contemporary Images of Christian Ministry* (Nashville: Abingdon Press, 1989), 162.

[6]Center for Catholic and Evangelical Theology, Summer, 1998.

[7]Ephesians 2:19–20.

[8]Douglas John Hall, *Confessing the Faith* (Minneapolis: Fortress Press, 1996), 84.

[9]Victor Hoagland, *The Book of Saints* (New York: Regina Press, 1986), 225.

[10]Hall, *Confessing the Faith*, 72.

[11]The Confessing Church was that community of German Evangelical Christians who opposed the German Christian Movement sponsored by the Nazi regime between 1934 and 1945.

[12]Hall, *Confessing the Faith*.

[13]2 Corinthians 4:5.

[14]This phrase comes from a story about Anna Freud during the blitz in London. She found a child running down the street during a bombing raid. She scooped up the terrified child in her arms and asked him his name. He could not remember it and said, "I guess I am nobody's nothing." I heard this story related by Ernest T. Campbell when I was a student at Union Theological Seminary.

[15]The Barmen Declaration was formulated in Barmen, Germany, at the first synod of the Confessing Church in Germany. Its purpose was to help define the belief and mission of the church in the face of the rise of Nazi Germany and the acquiescence of the German Christians to Nazi influence and power.

[16]Said by Carlyle Marney to a group of pastors gathered in retreat at Interpreters House, Lake Junaluska, North Carolina.

[17]*The Book of Common Prayer* (New York: The Church Hymnal Corporation, 1979), 149.

[18]John Snow, *The Impossible Vocation* (Boston: Cowley Press, 1988), 22.

[19]These five dilemmas were initially articulated by my close friend and ministerial colleague Rev. Dr. James W. Hulsey during a retreat we led on the pastoral vocation at A Mountain Retreat in Colorado. Dr. Hulsey is pastor of First Presbyterian Church, Smithtown, New York.

[20]See Jacques Barzun, *From Dawn to Decadence: 500 Years of Western Cultural Life* (New York: HarperCollins, 2000).

[21]Hall, *Confessing the Faith*, 196.

[22]Diogenes Allen, *Spiritual Theology* (Boston: Cowley Press, 1997), 2.

Chapter 2: Compasses and the Journey

[1]Frederick Buechner, *Wishful Thinking* (London: Collins, 1973), 95.

[2]From G. Edwin Osborn, ed., *Christian Worship: A Service Book* (St. Louis: Bethany Press, 1953). Reaffirmed in Colbert S. Cartwright and O. I. Cricket Harrison, eds., *Chalice Worship* (St. Louis: Chalice Press, 1997).

[3]From *Service of Consecration and Ordination*, United Methodist Church.

[4]From *A Service of Ordination to the Ministry of Word and Sacrament*. Prepared by the Occasional Services Task Force, Presbyterian Church (USA). Constitutional questions for those being ordained to the ministry of word and sacrament.

[5]From *Occasional Services: A Companion to Lutheran Book of Worship* (Minneapolis: Augsburg Publishing House; Philadelphia: Board of Publication, Lutheran Church in America).

Chapter 3: Clarity and Ten Theses

[1]Martin Luther, *Luther's Works,* vol. 41 (Philadelphia: Fortress Press, 1963), 148–65.

[2]I am indebted to my friend and colleague in ministry the Reverend Phillip Max Johnson for formulating the essential content of these ten theses while we were leading a vocational retreat with pastors at A Mountain Retreat. Rev. Johnson is pastor of St. Paul's Lutheran Church in Jersey City, New Jersey, and the Senior of the Society of the Holy Trinity. He is my former colleague at Disciples House in London, England.

[3]*Luther's Works,* 148–65.

[4]Henri J. M. Nouwen, *In the Name of Jesus* (New York: Crossroad, 2000), 17, 22.

[5]Charles E. Hummel, *The Tyranny of the Urgent* (Downer's Grove, Ill.: InterVarsity Press, 1999).

[6]Abraham Heschel, "The Jewish Notion of God," in *Theology of Renewal,* ed. L. K. Shook, 2 vols. (New York: Herder and Herder, 1968), 1:115.

[7]Frank C. Senn, *Christian Liturgy: Catholic and Evangelical* (Minneapolis: Fortress Press, 1997), xiv.

[8]Quoted in Murdo Ewen MacDonald, *The Call To Obey* (London: Hodder and Stoughton, 1963), 162.

Chapter 4: Creativity: Images and Imagination

[1]Paul Minear, *Images of the Church* (Philadelphia: Westminster Press, 1960).

[2]Ibid., 23.

[3]Ibid., 24.

[4]Ibid., 25.

[5]Urban T. Holmes III, *Ministry and Imagination* (New York: Seabury Press, 1981).

[6]Eugene H. Peterson, *The Contemplative Pastor* (Grand Rapids, Mich.: Eerdmans, 1989).

[7]Letty Russell, *Church in the Round* (Louisville: Westminster/John Knox Press, 1993).

[8]Donald E. Messer, *Contemporary Images of Christian Ministry* (Nashville: Abingdon Press, 1989).

[9]Henri Nouwen, *In the Name of Jesus* (New York: Crossroad, 2000).

[10]Minear, *Images of the Church.*

[11]Avery Dulles, *Models of the Church* (New York: Image Books, 1987).

[12]Sallie McFague, *The Body of God* (Minneapolis: Fortress Press, 1993).

[13]Russell, *Church in the Round.*

[14]Victor L. Hunter and Phillip Johnson, *The Human Church in the Presence of Christ: The Congregation Rediscovered* (Macon, Ga.: Mercer University Press, 1985).

[15]Holmes, *Ministry and Imagination.*

[16]Marcus J. Borg, *Jesus in Contemporary Scholarship* (Harrisburg, Pa.: Trinity Press International, 1994).

Chapter 5: Confessions and Theological Foundations

[1]Eugene Peterson, *Under the Unpredictable Plant* (Grand Rapids, Mich.: Eerdmans, 1992), 4.

[2]See Daniel Migliore, *The Power of God* (Philadelphia: Westminster Press, 1983). I am indebted to Migliore for his use of these terms. My interest in their use is their implications for the understanding of the pastoral vocation and its relationship to issues of power and authority.

³Carlyle Marney, *Priests to Each Other* (Valley Forge, Pa.: Judson Press, 1974), 7–8.

⁴Habakkuk 2:18–20.

⁵2 Corinthians 4:7; 3:5–6a.

⁶See Luke 4:16ff.

⁷Parker J. Palmer, *Let Your Life Speak: Listening to the Voice of Vocation* (San Francisco: Jossey-Bass, 2000).

⁸Marney, *Priests to Each Other,* 34.

⁹Corbin Scott Carnell, *Bright Shadow of Reality: C. S. Lewis and the Feeling Intellect* (Grand Rapids, Mich.: Eerdmans, 1974), 163, quoted in Eugene H. Peterson, *Five Smooth Stones for Pastoral Work* (Atlanta: John Knox Press, 1980), 63.

¹⁰Martin Buber, *The Way of Man* (Secaucus, N.J.: Citadel Press, 1966), 17.

¹¹Eugene Peterson, *The Contemplative Pastor* (Grand Rapids, Mich.: Eerdmans, 1989), 19–21.

¹²Marney, *Priests to Each Other,* 41.

¹³Abraham Joshua Heschel, *Man Is Not Alone* (New York: Farrar, Straus and Giroux, 1951), 161.

¹⁴Nihls Dahl, "Anamnesis: Memory and Commemoration in Early Christianity," *Studia Theologica* 1 (1947): 75.

¹⁵Henri J. M. Nouwen, *The Living Reminder* (Minneapolis: Seabury Press, 1977), 13.

¹⁶John 16:33.

¹⁷Quoted in Marney, *Priests to Each Other,* 31.

¹⁸Ibid.

Chapter 6: A *Regula Pastorum* for Contemporary Pastors

¹Matthew 11:30: "My yoke is easy, and my burden is light."

²Albert Curry Winn, "The Plainest and Simplest Thing in the World," in *To God Be The Glory: Sermons in Honor of George Arthur Buttrick,* ed. Theodore A. Gill (New York: Abingdon Press, 1973), 127.

³Augustine, *Sermon LXXIII* (*Sermon CXXIII* in the Benedictine text), "Sermons on Selected Lessons of the New Testament," trans. R. G. MacMullen, in *The Nicene and Post-Nicene Fathers of the Christian Church,* ed. Philip Schaff (Edinburgh: T&T Clark, 1887; reprint, Grand Rapids, Mich.: Eerdmans, 1991), 473–74.

⁴This poem is a paraphrase from W. H. Auden's "In Memory of W. B. Yeats," copyright 1940 and renewed 1968 by W. H. Auden, from *W. H. Auden: The Collected Poems,* ed. Edward Mendelson (New York: Random House, 1976).

Chapter 7: The Pastor under Many and Varied Conditions

¹Reinhold Niebuhr, *Leaves from the Notebook of a Tamed Cynic* (New York: Meridian Books, 1929), 18.

²See Richard H. Lowery, *Sabbath and Jubilee,* Understanding Biblical Themes (St. Louis: Chalice Press, 2000), for a creative discussion of the Sabbath and its implications for our spiritual, economic, and social life.

³Mark 2:27.

⁴Walter Brueggemann and George W. Stroup, eds., *Many Voices, One God: Being Faithful in a Pluralistic World. Essays in Honor of Shirley Guthrie* (Louisville: Westminster John Knox Press, 1998), 193.

⁵Isaiah 55:1–3.

Chapter 8: The Pastor and Worship

¹Matthew 18:20.

²Acts 2:42.

³Hebrews 10:24–25.

⁴Ignatius, *Ephesians,* 5:2.

⁵See Frank C. Senn, *Christian Liturgy: Catholic and Evangelical* (Minneapolis: Fortress Press, 1997), for a sweeping but detailed history of liturgy and its

relationship to culture and cultural needs for the expression and celebration of the story of Jesus of Nazareth.

⁶Translation: "The way you pray influences what you believe, what you believe influences the way you pray."

⁷Alister E. McGrath, *Christian Theology: An Introduction* (Oxford: Blackwell, 1994), 191.

⁸Senn, *Christian Liturgy,* 8.

⁹Ibid.

¹⁰Quoted in Senn, *Christian Liturgy,* 9.

¹¹Ibid. The term *liminal* is derived from the Latin *limen* ("threshold").

¹²1 Corinthians 11:23–25.

¹³I use "bait and switch" to describe the approach to evangelism that lures people in with some exciting, entertaining, or attractive offering, with the plan to then switch them to some form of church membership or discipleship.

¹⁴1 Corinthians 11:27–32.

¹⁵*Manual of Prayers* (Washington, D. C.: Pontifical North American College, 1998).

¹⁶Deuteronomy 6:4–5.

¹⁷Michael Ramsey, Archbishop of Canterbury during the turbulent middle years of the last century, was asked by a group of ordinands how long he prayed each day. After a long pause he said, "Two minutes." The ordinands were shocked at this brevity. The Archbishop then went on, "But I prepare to pray for an hour. If I can then get two minutes of honest prayer, it's okay." This story was related to me by Ramsey's friend Rev. Dr. Kenneth Leech, Resident Theologian of St. Botolph's in London's East End.

¹⁸Dietrich Bonhoeffer, *Life Together,* trans. John W. Doberstein (New York: Harper and Row, 1954), 119.

¹⁹James 5:16.

²⁰Matthew 5:23–24.

²¹See Douglas John Hall, *God and Human Suffering: An Exercise in the Theology of the Cross* (Minneapolis: Augsburg, 1986). For a discussion of reactions to suffering in communities of affluence, see Victor L. Hunter, *Pedagogy of the Prosperous* (Unpublished D.Min. Project, Phillips Theological Seminary, 1995).

²²Irvin D. Yalom, *When Nietzche Wept* (Hamburg: Kabel Verlag, 1994).

²³Mark 15:34.

²⁴Isaiah 53:5; 1 Peter 2:23.

Chapter 9: The Pastor with the People

¹Quoted in Bennett J. Sims, *Servanthood* (Cambridge: Cowley Publications, 1997), 3.

²Paulo Friere, *Pedagogy of the Oppressed,* twentieth anniversary ed., trans. Myra Bergman Ramos (New York: Continuum, 1993), 52. The banking method of education is where all authority and knowledge are presumed to be in the teacher, and the teacher makes "intellectual" deposits into the educational accounts of the objects of education.

³Carl Rogers, *On Becoming a Person: A Therapist's View of Psychotherapy* (New York: Houghton-Mifflin, 1961), 32.

⁴Roy Herndon SteinhoffSmith, *The Mutuality of Care* (St. Louis: Chalice Press, 1999).

⁵See my discussion of boundaries in chapter 3.

⁶Frederick Buechner, *Telling Secrets* (San Francisco: HarperSanFrancisco, 1991).

⁷Frederick Buechner, *Telling the Truth: The Gospel as Tragedy, Comedy and Fairy Tale* (San Francisco: Harper and Row, 1977).

⁸Source unknown.

⁹Quoted in George Gilder, *Wealth and Poverty* (New York: Basic Books, 1981), 268–69.

¹⁰Original source unknown. The Romero reflection was sent to me by my regional minister.

[11]Friedrich Nietzsche, *The Portable Nietzsche*, ed. W. Kaufmann (New York: Viking Press, 1965), 204.
[12]See William A. Clebsch and Charles Jaekle, *Pastoral Care in Historical Perspective* (New York: Jason Aronson, 1983).
[13]Luke 6:39, paraphrased.
[14]2 Corinthians 5:18–20.
[15]2 Corinthians 4:7.

Chapter 10: The Pastor and Christian Community

[1]See Hans Kung, *The Church* (New York: Image Books, 1976), 169–77.
[2]George Lindbeck, *Christian Century*, May 7, 1990.
[3]Douglas John Hall, *The End of Christendom and the Future of Christianity* (Harrisburg, Pa.: Trinity Press, 1995).
[4]See Richard H. Lowery, *Sabbath and Jubilee*, Understanding Biblical Themes (St. Louis: Chalice Press, 2000).
[5]The epistle of 1 John continually circles this theme of attentiveness to and love of God and attentiveness to and love of the sister or brother. It is, of course, a reflection of the great commandment on loving God and loving neighbor.
[6]Antoine de Saint-Exupéry, *The Little Prince*, trans. Katherine Woods (New York: Harcourt, Brace and World, 1943), 83–84.
[7]Cited in C. S. Lewis, *A Mind Awake*, ed. Clyde S. Kelly (New York: Harcourt Brace Jovanovich, 1968), 191.
[8]Douglas John Hall, *God and Human Suffering* (Minneapolis: Augsburg, 1986).
[9]Gunther Grass, *The Tin Drum*, trans. Ralph Manheim (New York: Pantheon, 1961), 525.

Chapter 11: The Pastor as Leader and Administrator

[1]1 Corinthians 12:28.
[2]Mark 10:35–45.
[3]Alvin J. Lindgren, *Foundations for Purposeful Church Administration* (Nashville: Abingdon Press, 1965), 60.
[4]Quoted in *Great Quotes from Great Leaders* (Lombard, Ill.: Celebrating Excellence Publishing, 1990), 33.
[5]Ibid., 101.
[6]Ibid., 123.
[7]Ibid., 85.
[8]Ibid., 3.
[9]This illustration and the seven principles regarding the New York Orpheus were drawn from a report I heard on National Public Radio.
[10]Nancy Fuchs-Kreimer, "Holiness, Justice and the Rabbinate," *CrossCurrents: The Journal of the Association for Religion and Intellectual Life* 42 (Summer 1992): 212–13.
[11]Ibid., 224.

Chapter 12: The Pastor's Survival Kit

[1]Thomas Groome, *Christian Religious Education* (San Francisco: HarperCollins, 1980).
[2]Ibid., 137.
[3]Donald P. Smith, *Clergy in the Crossfire: Coping with Role Conflicts in the Ministry* (Philadelphia: Westminster Press, 1974).
[4]Dietrich Bonhoeffer, *Letters and Papers from Prison*, ed. Eberhard Bethge, trans. Reginald H. Fuller (London: SCM Press, 1956), 165.
[5]Maya Angelou, *The Complete Collected Poems of Maya Angelou* (New York: Random House, 1994), 74.